IT'S YOUR CHOICE

Your Practical Guide to
Achieving Lasting Satisfaction in Your
Personal and Professional Life!

JACK GALLAGHER

IT'S YOUR CHOICE

TABLE OF CONTENTS

This book is for all those people out there who are looking for real lasting success and happiness.

Based on the author's experiences, training, and insights, it provides a step by step guide to self-discovery and how to understand and appreciate those things that truly make you happy and successful throughout your entire life.

It is filled with light hearted insights, thoughtful stories of rising above challenges, and practical exercises for the reader's participation.

Enjoy the journey to success and happiness.

"It's Your Choice" is a practical book filled with tools and strategies to begin transforming your life from the inside out. From strengthening your mind to building a sustainable financial plan, this book can help you get from Point A - where you are, to Point B - where you want to go. This book is for anyone wanting more satisfaction in their personal and professional lives!

…Robin B. O'Grady, Author of "The Optimist's Edge: Moving Beyond Negativity to Create Your Amazing Life"

Jack's Life experiences lend him unique insights to finding success and happiness. "It's Your Choice" is a MUST read!

…Barbara Murray, Author of "Taking Back Parenting: Giving Your Children What They Need from You to Succeed in Life"

FORWARD

Within these pages, Jack shares some of his most personal experiences and lessons learned from his life. Starting with his boyhood in a neglectful alcoholic family to his activities during the Cold War, and his eventual understanding of love and the real meaning of success.

His intent with this book is to help others who might be searching for their own identity and happiness. Jack defines "success" very differently from most others. He views it as being free from the influence of others' expectations of what you "should" do. In fact, he hates being told he "should" do this or that. Advice is welcomed but he has learned to decide for himself. It took him many years to get to that point. And he adds the word "happiness" as essential to his definition of success.

Jack's story isn't one of rising from a ghetto or earning millions of dollars or even owning his own business. It is a story of observations of life, introspection, a burning desire to simply understand, and, finally, to be himself when there was nobody to guide him. And he did.

Jack is the third of four children, born within a month of his older sister's death at the age of three. His older brother was a bitter alcoholic who died prematurely at the age of fifty-five, in large part due to his choice of life style. He was simply a very angry man, married four times, and spent his life looking for revenge. Jack never understood why his brother was like that.

Jack also has a younger sister who grew up pretty much neglected, as did Jack. She supports and loves her family but also struggles to understand her life.

Jack's parents had to marry in a day when such marriages were expected when there was an unexpected child involved (Jack's brother). They could not have been much different from each other and it cannot be said that they shared the same views of life or even of living together. Jack's father was a blue collar, tough guy who worked in the rail yards and docks of Buffalo, New York. He was the oldest son in a large family and supported his family from the time he was about sixteen years old. He was a drinker, an athlete, a great story teller, and was well known and welcomed throughout the city. He was also an abusive alcoholic.

Jack's mother was a pampered child and the youngest in a large family. She became the youngest when her younger sibling died, also as a young child. His mother expected a genteel life but got a rough and tumble tough guy instead. She never forgave him or accepted him. She ended up simply staring out a window and lived most of her life inside her own make believe world.

This kind of family left Jack to his own devices, almost from the moment he was born. Nobody ever guided him as a child. Nobody ever held him in their arms and told him he was loved or even valued in any way. This led to Jack's sense of isolation, suspicion of others, and put him on a path to alcoholism.

But something always told Jack this was not right. He will tell you he kept searching and trying to understand what was "right." He found it. And he is sharing his discovery for others who may be searching also.

Jack lives in the Puget Sound area on the Olympic Peninsula and has been happily married to his wife for going on fifty years. Together, they have three successful adult children and four grandchildren. He served in the US Air Force during the Vietnam War and Cold War era, several of those years flying top secret spy missions for the CIA. He dropped out of college after two years but finished his undergraduate degree in Business some years later and went on to earn his Masters Degree in Business, emphasizing organizational and management leadership.

Jack has helped a number of individuals, organizations, and businesses "find" themselves and change their lives for the better. This is what he does best.

He mostly enjoys family time, hiking, reading, and photography. He'll tell you with a smile that he enjoys a fine glass of wine also.

INTRODUCTION

First off, I have to tell you to not buy this book if you're really not serious about putting at least some effort into making lasting changes in your life, achieving goals, or just becoming really happy and content with yourself.

Why? Because this is no "7 STEPS TO HAPPINESS," or "YOU IN 4 WEEKS," kind of book. Those are great and if you want some gems to consider put this book down now and keep looking. Oh, there are clearly gems in this book too but the point of view is different from the others on the shelf. This book is filled with thoughts, ideas, and techniques that I've learned over a life time. And my life time started out without much prospect for real success. No, it wasn't the worst way to start but it wasn't the greatest either. The techniques I've learned I'm passing on to you for your benefit.

This book is intended for those of you who are maybe struggling or even living your life pretty normally but you are looking for something more. You want to get it right and feel fulfilled, but you don't. You wonder if you are really living your life to its fullest. You worry about your future. You worry about making the wrong decisions. You wonder if you can make it. You wonder what others see in you and how they are judging you. You reach for success but it seems to elude you somehow. And you keep searching.

You don't feel like you fit in but you want to. You are uncertain. You may ask why others seem so much more successful or so much happier or just more confident than you. Why can't you feel the way the others seem to feel?

I have answers and can guide you to your personal success. I learned the hard way without much help and suffered a lot of mistakes along the way that you don't need to. I'm hoping that you learn from the lessons I've learned and begin to enjoy your own success without so many mistakes and lost time. I want you to get out there with confidence, achieve what you desire, and know what it's like to simply enjoy your life. It's out there waiting for you. I believe that sincerely.

It's going to take some work first though. If you are really tired of trying and not getting what you want, or not even sure of what you want in the long run, and you're really willing to work on this for the long haul, then this might be a worthwhile book for you.

Real change takes time. Real accomplishment takes planning. Success and happiness take work. You have to be in it for the long term and you have to do work throughout this book. Some of that work, heck, maybe a lot of it, will be difficult to do if you're totally honest with yourself. It will be especially difficult if you're not accustomed to looking inside your own mind and examining what you do, how you think, and why you do what you do.

You will have to face your reality. That means all the good and the bad stuff you have locked up inside of you. For some, that can be painful. On top of that, there are action exercises that you must do. And you must be persistent at those. This book will not be easy and it will take time. Have I made that clear yet?

How is this book different? I'll tell you.

I have read almost all the self-help books out there. I've attended workshops and support groups to help find my way. I've lived my life at so many different levels that I feel like I can relate to almost anyone and almost any situation. I understand. I've scrubbed floors, loaded and unloaded trucks by hand, and stocked shelves. I've also been a manager most of my working life so I've read most of the management books too. You know, all about how to deal with difficult people, how to improve your productivity, even those about how to get rich investing in real estate. (I have made a fair amount of money doing that and I like to think I was an effective manager and leader.) I've been in the military, done sales, finance, logistics, leadership, strategic planning, coaching, consulting, and more.

The point is this: It seems to me that almost every one of those books, workshops, motivational speakers, etc., I've experienced over the years has defined "success" as either the achievement of a goal or the making a lot of money. But they have left something out. They give great tidbits and they certainly are motivating. They are also really helpful on particular subjects.

So what are they missing?

I have never seen anything that puts the whole person together. And I really mean change or achievement from the inside out – the whole "you." The trend that I've observed is the outward achievement of goals rather than the personal, internal satisfaction of daily achievement of life in general. I define success differently and, I believe, more comprehensively, more internal, more personal.

So many people do achieve the goals of making lots of money, becoming great leaders, losing that gut, and all the other stuff one might pursue. But too many of those same people have weird kids, or are so self-centered and protective of their fragile egos that you can’t even joke with them and have some fun. They’re wound up so tight you fear they will pop and violently uncoil right in front of you one day. These people live for their work and define themselves by their jobs, or their wealth, or their status – yeah, and end up divorced, kids on drugs, heart patients, generally whacko, or whatever.

We are overwhelmed by images of what others think we should be. We see ads in print, on television, on our personal devices; almost everywhere we turn. There are whole marketing divisions that are turning to the use of neurological sciences to understand how to persuade us to think a certain way or buy a certain product. This goes beyond mere influence. To me it takes away your freedom of choice when you can be manipulated so much and so often. The “you” disappears and is replaced by conditioned responses.

If that sounds over the top, look around one day and count how many times you see an ad. In fact, try to count how many times you see an ad for just one type of product, say food. How about automobiles?

Of course, certainly not everyone succumbs to every attempt to sway his or her thinking. But, to me anyway, it seems to be too many. How happy are you really? Are you successfully being yourself in life or are you playing the role of someone you think you should be? Do you fear you will lose it all one day and have restless, sleepless nights because of your worries? Do you think you’ve failed if you don’t own a mansion, a limo, go to parties in formal wear, or appear on the cover of "Time Magazine," "Rolling Stone," or whatever success publication you may envy?

I grew up in a highly dysfunctional, alcoholic family so I was pretty messed up. Mostly from pure neglect. I was a kid who was blessed though with some sense that this was all wrong but I had no idea what was "right" or "normal." I longed to be like the other kids but I knew deep down I wasn't. It took me years to figure out what it was and it also took a lot of patience and love from my wife and children to help me finally figure it all out. It did take all that training and all those books and it took patient, caring friends.

The answer to real success in life is pretty simple: Be you. Getting there is really hard if you don't have help. Help starts with "Who are you?" And, I like to think it ends with a happy smile and a good night's sleep. Throw in self-confidence too and the world is yours.

That's what this book is all about. It is the work of self-discovery, but so are many other books. This one shows you how to not only get there but also guides you through the entire process from wherever you might be now to wherever it is you want to be or whatever it is you want to achieve. It's the whole enchilada. And it's also plain, simple, and basic in order to make the whole thing as easy as possible for you to follow and accomplish and get results.

Ok, so why am I writing this book? First, it seems to me there is a need for it. Our society is pretty messed up in a lot of ways. I've already commented on my view of marketing and I'll show you some examples in the pages that follow.

I believe the United States is the greatest country in the world but I see too many seeds of its demise as we've known it. Too much of the world hates us and we are under attack. We have the greatest concentration of wealth in the world yet we have high rates of homelessness. People are losing their homes and their businesses and jobs. The middle class backbone of our country is eroding rapidly. Our healthcare system is a wreck. Our government is becoming more and more ineffective. Why? Lots of reasons but I believe mostly that we've generally lost our way. We are more and more a society of "one size fits all." Americanism used to mean fierce individuality joined by vast opportunity.

We are becoming a welfare state with too many individuals dependent upon "the system." We've come to accept that and generally feel "entitled." And, bottom line, we individuals have become complacent. COMPLACENT!! PASSIVE!! LET SOMEONE ELSE DO IT FOR US OR JUST FORGET ABOUT IT!! Is this really the way we want to live? I say…

NO!

Better yet…

HELL NO!

So let's do something about it. Let's find yourself and get going on your journey to being you – active, thoughtful, achieving, happy, and satisfied you.

This is not your average motivational stuff. This is a workbook of a unique style based on sound practices and experiences. Ready to do some work? Ok, then turn the page and we'll start.

I sincerely hope you get something really valuable out of these pages; something that will help you find yourself and confidently be the person you really are. I know you can find the success and happiness you have a right to enjoy. You have a choice!

Jack

PART ONE
How This Book Works

This book is a combination of a life story, a journey, some philosophy, workbook exercises, and advice based on a lot of different sources and almost seven decades of education and personal experiences. I don't expect anyone to agree with everything within these pages. I also don't expect everyone to do all the exercises suggested but I do recommend you do as many as possible in order to get the most benefit from these pages. Just don't skip over things because they might be difficult. If you do you will not get the benefit of what these pages hold for you. It's a process.

This book is produced in both paperback and in e-formats. So if you are using an electronic format, when you come to exercises on pages provided as in a workbook, please don't use any indelible marker on your e-format page. It will be just a mess and probably too small to read anyway. But please do use some paper and follow the formats provided. Yeah, it's old fashioned but it will work.

If you have purchased this book in paperback use the pages provided and always feel free to use some additional paper if that suits you better.

You, the reader, get to pick what fits and is best for you. This whole book is intended to be a series of eye opening introspections to help you define in real terms who you really are and what it is that defines you. You don't need to spend too much time on any one thing but do spend at least some on it and then just move along to the next. If something seems stupid or too challenging, then please give it a try anyway. I strongly urge you to spend some time on it as it might just open your mind some and you might find a surprise inside. If something rings a bell, go with it. This book is really all about you and for your benefit.

Now, I don't know you and have never met you. So you probably are asking yourself, how can I presume to advise you at all?

The answer to that is because I've found my way through a lot of bullshit, lies, misinformation, ignorance, cruelty, and indifference to arrive at a place where I can deal with all the crap in the world and still find real success, happiness, and contentment in the simplest things and especially in work, family, and community. Instead of blindly following the dangerous path to destruction that I was on, I have learned how to build a new path, a better way. And I can show you how to do the same too.

What I've learned over a lifetime (I was born in 1946 by the way so any of you who don't want to listen to my "Boomer" generation's experiences can put this back on the shelf now before you reach the check out.) I'm sharing with you, but only if you want it. And it's a lot.

For some reason, I was born with a knack for really pissing people off. My Mother told me I used to scream for hours as a baby and kick until my heels bled. Nothing could satisfy me. So started my life. Unsatisfied.

When I got older I questioned everything. Yeah, in a world where kids were to be seen and not heard, I would join the adult conversations and ask "Why?" I seldom got any kind of answer at my young age. So I had to figure things out for myself. It took a long time but I found a lot of very predictable patterns in people's behavior. I learned to watch, to listen, and to read things like the dictionary, history books, the encyclopedia, and a lot about World War II.

I read about victory, luck, planning, and real heroes. I read about differences in people and places. I read about chance success and planned success. I saw pictures of the horrors that some people can inflict on others. And I listened to the adults talk about money, family, work, politics, and a lot of bullshit. I saw people pretend to be other than they were. I saw drunken parties, gambling, auto accidents, arguments, and dissatisfied miserable "grown-ups."

People and organizations all seemed to be simply existing and repeating the same trite conversations over and over with no real growth, success, or happiness. They all seemed "stuck" to me. Made from some invisible cookie cutter. Nobody seemed to be going anywhere with their lives. Be born, grow up learning the same things your parents believed, get a job, get married, have kids, raise them to be just like you, then get old and die. Repeat. And repeat again. Why? It made no sense when I was very young. It still doesn't.

Somehow, I found my way out of the mysterious woods that were my family and my schools, and my neighborhood. What I've learned is basically this: You have to know and understand yourself above all other things. That is not an easy thing if you are really honest with yourself and willing to question almost everything around you. I'll show you why and I'll take you through a series of steps, the first of which will show you how to prepare to question yourself and your surroundings.

Before you do any mental and emotional heavy lifting you have to prepare your mind to see yourself as you really are. Only after that will we really begin.

This book builds on itself slowly but surely until, in the end, you will have all the tools necessary to understand who you really are, what and why you want what you want, how to think for yourself and not be led by others' influences over you. You will learn how to make your own decisions for your own good and for the benefit of those who are close to you. And you will learn how to simply be a positive influence in general. You will learn how to make action oriented decisions that move you to a better place or help you achieve your goals or get that cool car you really, honestly want. You will learn to build a better view of yourself and your world.

And you will fail occasionally along the way but you will understand why failure can benefit you and how you can get right back up and press on with a smile on your face and an even clearer image of your strengths and capabilities. You will learn how to deal with setbacks, and those negative people we seem to be surrounded by sometimes, including bully bosses or those toxic people at work or in your social group. Maybe even someone in your family. Maybe your own thoughts of yourself.

We'll deal with complacency by showing you how to tap into your energy and how to recharge yourself when you do run low. And I do mean totally positive energy that will keep you going, and going, and going happily. Unlike the fuzzy pink bunny, your energy will be real; not just an ad to sell something.

And, this is not a fairy tale kind of book. It is not all smiles and “have a nice day” dreamy view of the world kind of book either. I know what it is like to totally flop at things. I’ve been fired, I’ve been shot at, I’ve had bad performance reviews, I’ve had fights and arguments, been beaten up and knocked down. I’ve had about the crappiest bosses you could imagine too and some pretty bad employees along the way. More than one threatened to kill me! My own father once picked me up by the throat in a fury over a high school football game. Nice father/son bonding moment, huh? In all fairness to my father though, I’ve come to understand just how great a guy he really was and how totally frustrated he was with me. More about all that later.

Clearly, this is not a perfect world! You already know that. But it is the one we live in so we have to learn to deal with it. I will show you how to do that so that you come out ahead in the end – maybe with a black eye or even a scar (Sorry, but there is real danger in the world.). However, you will have the tools to deal with those things too.

Given all the crap I grew up with, but blessed with a lot of natural insight and curiosity, and later given the gift of more love and support than I could ever hope for from my wife in particular, I also achieved an MBA, helped raise three very independent and successful children, have a long and happy marriage, have made significant contributions to my professional field, received a bunch of awards and accolades, have a few very close friends, made a pretty good income, have virtually everything I could ever want, and I’m a really happy and contented guy.

You can achieve your dreams too. And you can make those dreams stick. You can have a better life!

Finally, and maybe most importantly, you will learn how to build on your successes and (here's the biggest part that's missing in most other books) how to sustain your achievements. I will give you realistic tools to do this; simple tools you can apply over and over again. My gift to you.

But, remember, you have to get engaged with all this. This is not a book of do step one, then step two, etc., and just leave it at that. This is more like weaving a tapestry or adding pixels a handful at a time. A pattern evolves eventually that is a part of the whole thing. Each of these lessons or shared experiences does that. They build together to form a successful model for you.

And that's how the whole thing works: slowly over time, one achievement or one insight at a time. You will (I really expect) have a number of "Ah Ha" moments as you weave your way through this book of exploration and learning about yourself.

Frankly, some of it might scare you. Some may upset you. Some may pull up old buried memories you might prefer to leave in the closet of your soul. Remember, I have a talent for pissing people off because I tend to look really closely at the wounds and I might even scratch at them. I do believe that if you ignore the bullshit in your life and bury it, it doesn't really go away. Best to get it out into the daylight, look closely at it, understand why it affects you, and then put it in its proper perspective. We are all made of nice stuff and stuff that tends to stink. Let the air and sunshine do its thing.

OK? So now you have an idea how this will work. I'll lead you through a series of exercises and stories that show you how to open your mind to change. Then I'll show you techniques to understand the real reasons you want the things you believe you want. I'll show you how to make changes that really will improve you or your situation based on who you are and what you value. I'll show you how to recognize and address the dangers along the way. And, in the end, I'll show you how to put it all together so it isn't just a cool thing to have read, fills you with great hope and inspiration, then just sits on a shelf in your room somewhere, neglected until the next garage sale.

Hopefully, this is something you will go through, learn, pull out again from time to time and find it useful as you enjoy the good things in your life and deal with the crap that may come your way.

PART TWO
STRENGTHENING YOUR MIND

Wow! You're still reading! Congratulations!

Well let's get right to it, ok?

In this Part I'm going to show you a couple very basic things about how your mind works. You function in this world by using two basic tools: Perceptions and Habits. Your mind interprets all the input around you and you develop habits around those perceptions.

BIG CAUTION HERE: Both can be dead wrong!

How Perceptions Work

Do you remember the cartoon “Peanuts?” All the children (and Snoopy) hear is gibberish when adults speak. Muted Blah, Blah, Blah. They speak to each other clearly and Snoopy doesn’t even speak to the children. He only thinks but can have conversations with the little bird. Without realizing it, we sometimes do the same things.

We can tune people out when we don’t think they are important. Or we can become so engrossed in what we are doing, focused so much on something else, that we don’t even hear someone approaching or talking to us. We honestly don’t hear what they say. On the other hand, we may think we understand what people are thinking because, I guess, we think we can read minds. We will actually interpret others’ words differently than what they really said because we already believe we know what they are saying. Isn’t that amazing? But we do it all the time!

Has anyone ever said to you, “That’s not at all what I said.”? Have you ever been in a room with the television on but never had a clue what was on, let alone what was being said? Have you ever finished someone’s sentence for them believing you know what they are going to say only to be wrong?

My wife is an avid reader. She can be so focused on what she is reading that I can actually stand right next to her, speak several sentences of something I think is very important, then walk away believing I’ve clearly and effectively communicated with her in some meaningful way. Very pleased with myself that I have “communicated.” Moments later she will have absolutely no recollection that I was even in the room, right next to her. Needless to say, she didn’t even hear me – not a word! Of course, I always hear every word she tells me (but please don’t ask her about that).

Real communication is a two-way deal. A message is sent out from source “A” and received by recipient “B.” The process requires that the message be translated from A to B though in some manner that has the intended meaning that A sent out. This doesn’t always happen. The message gets lost (not received at all), or garbled (Blah, blah, blah), or mistranslated (the meaning is added to, subtracted from, or outright changed).

It seems children pick up on this and have learned this about us adults too. Kids are very smart because they haven’t learned the rules yet nor become corrupted by them. When do they ask for stuff? When we’re busy and preoccupied and tend to just say “Yes.”

“Jack, when did you tell our four year old daughter she could drive the car to the corner?”

“I never said that!”

“That’s not what she told me, Jack! ☹”

“Oh, yeah, I guess I did when I was engrossed in that football game. So where is she? Hell, where’s the car? Why is there a police car in front of the house? Is she ok?”

This may be a bit extreme. At least I hope so! But you get the picture. I never heard her (but I sure heard all about it later!)

Have you ever seen the video of the people passing the basketball? If not look it up on YouTube. As the people pass the basketball, try to count how many times it passes from one particular person to another. If you haven’t seen it look it up now because once I tell you about it you won’t get the point. Stop and count now.

Go to your computer’s search engine and search “Basketball Gorilla.” Follow the directions.

Do this now before proceeding to the next page.

Ok, did you count how many times the ball passed between the players? Did you see the gorilla? Maybe you did, wise, observant person that you are, but most people will say, "Huh? What gorilla?" It's kind of hard to miss a gorilla but most people do when they are concentrating on something else and they are not expecting to see a gorilla. How can you NOT see a gorilla? For those of you who didn't see it, I even put the word "gorilla" in the computer search. In fact, in most versions of this video, the gorilla actually handles the ball or waves at you. Yeah! Go look again and you'll see what I'm talking about.

When you think about the fact we sometimes only see what we expect to see, you can also realize that what we see can dictate what we don't see. So, we don't always see or hear what's right in front of us. It simply doesn't register in our minds. Our minds are not capable of taking in everything that is presented to us. In other words, we filter information. Sometimes we fill in the blanks. And we tend to filter out the unexpected or those things we think are unimportant. Magicians rely on this function of our brains. It's simply how we're made. It's our mental wiring.

That's the first thing to recognize: we don't see everything that's happening around us. We fool ourselves to only see what's important or in the "now" for us. Pretty good evolutionary tool when we needed to focus on that saber tooth tiger that started chasing us.

But how well does it serve us today? Actually, pretty well. There is so much going on around us all the time now. We are bombarded with information visually, physically, and mentally. If we couldn't rely on our habits we would become paralyzed and unable to function. On the other hand, with so much going on to distract us, what are we missing? What are we misperceiving?

The other part of this perception thing is that we see what we expect to see (and hear). And if we tend to perceive what we already believe or expect to see, that tends to reinforce our biases; our already held beliefs. And that can just strengthen our misperceptions by reinforcing our patterns of beliefs, or habits.

Here's another example I've used for years. We all know what a square is, right? And I'm assuming you can count (based on the fact that you can read this). Ok, so count the squares in the diagram following. Then show it to a few other people and ask them to do the same. Here you go:

How many squares do you see?

Now, I realize you may have seen this before but even some who have still get it wrong. The obvious answer is 16 squares (4 across by 4 down). Oh, but then you realize the whole thing is also a square so the answer is 17. Clever! But wait a minute. What if I shaded some to make it appear differently? Same box, just shaded differently. Like this:

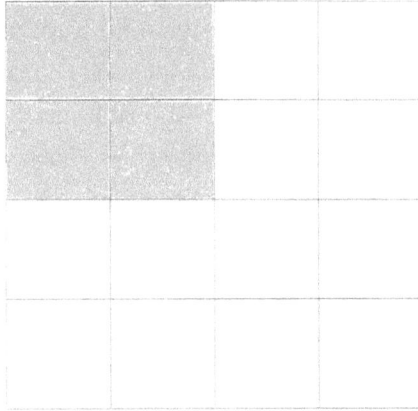

Well, that's another square! And you can probably see that there are four of these. So now the answer is 17 plus 4 more or 21. Wonderful! But wait a minute. There's more if I shade it differently again. Look at this:

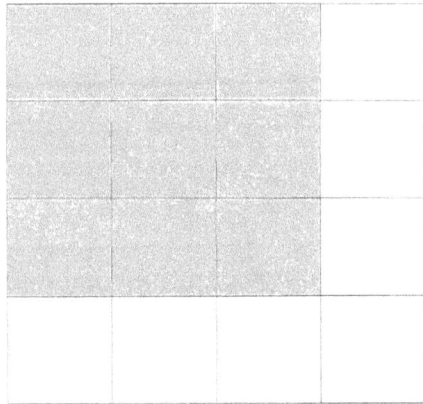

Now there is another square and you can move this square over one block to get another and down a block so you can get two more. So now we have 21 blocks plus 4 more, or 25 squares. Oh, my!

Now go back to the first blocks and look again. What if we moved that shaded block over one, then down one, and so on? We already counted four additional blocks in the corners. Now we can get 6 more! Wow! We now have 25 plus 6 more for 31 blocks! Thought you were pretty clever at some number less than that, huh? And if you did get them, that is pretty good as most people don't get it.

Now that I've written this and shown you that your initial perceptions can be wrong or, at best, incomplete, I have to go back and double check this myself to be sure I got it right. In other words, this doesn't come naturally even though I've used this example probably more than a hundred times to demonstrate to people that they cannot always count on their initial perception of even familiar things.

I'm sure you can think of things that you have seen, sworn you saw (or heard); only to find out you were wrong. It's like the eye witnesses to a crime who don't even come close to matching each other's sworn description of what happened, even down to the color of the criminal's skin, hair, or even sex. Amazing how we filter information to fit our mental predispositions.

There are a lot of optical illusions out there. Magicians rely on fooling your perceptions. The point is just to be aware that what you think you see or hear might not be correct.

Now Let's Talk About Habits

There's a really interesting book out there titled "The Power of Habit," by Charles Duhigg. In it he cites a number of studies about research done concerning habits and their cycles.

Basically, he describes some trigger that causes an action that produces a reward that reinforces the cycle to be repeated over and over. Each time it is repeated, and the reward is provided, the habit becomes stronger.

Remember when you were a kid learning to tie your shoes? OK, I learned in a pre-Velcro world so maybe this isn't a good example. How about the first time you drove a car? How about the first time you did anything? It wasn't easy, was it? You had to concentrate. You were clumsy. You failed probably many times. But, ever so slowly, you got better at it. You were driven to succeed either instinctively, like eating by yourself or maybe standing upright and walking, or by someone's encouragement.

Take a moment to think about all the things you do now without a thought. You brush your teeth, you get dressed, you can read, you do all sorts of things without any effort at all. We have wired our brains to do things automatically to the point at which we often don't even remember doing something that we did or, if asked how we do something, we're not sure.

Has anyone ever asked you how to do something you're good at and you forget the steps or stumble through an explanation? We rely on habits so that we don't have to figure things out each time we do them. Imagine if you had to think about how to tie your shoes or how to put your foot into a sock or even how to button a button. (Unless all your stuff is Velcro. ☺)

We learn by repetition and reward. And when we learn so well that something becomes automatic, we often become unaware that we are doing it or how we do it.

I grew up in New York State and people there talk really fast, tend to be aggressive, and use a lot of hand gestures. That's how it's done – there. When I was a department manager living in Montana, our organization started a team building program. Great! I was all for it and, in fact, had been developing my department along those very lines. I was training all my staff in communications, quality, teaching them stuff way beyond the minimums required to do their jobs. And they were great. What a team of such totally awesome, capable, dedicated, smart, happy employees. We were blowing the socks off all the other departments. I loved this team and could not have been prouder of each of them.

So, our team building facilitator schedules our team meeting and she placed me in the middle of the room surrounded by my fantastic staff. She began by asking the team what they thought of me. I'm good with that as I do believe in open communication and honesty. But what I got actually shocked me!

Their general consensus was that Jack was always pissed at them and didn't like them. Granted, he did a lot for them and they were a great team but why was Jack always angry with them?

Huh?

Holy crap! I was amazed and dumbfounded. Thanks for the feedback, team, but why do you think I'm pissed at you? The answer: "Because you're always yelling at us and waving your arms when you talk to us. It's very threatening!" What? Please tell me more because I don't yell at you and I'm not angry. Describe why you think this.

Ok. To me, normal speech is fast and loud and does include a lot of animated arm and even body movement. But that was ok "there" in New York and not ok "here" in Montana. Lesson learned. I was never aware of the differences in the way people communicated. So, I had to learn to slow down my speech, be a little quieter, and, for real, I began a habit of sitting on my hands during meetings. I wasn't aware I even did those things my staff was telling me and they were reacting to the signals I was sending out to them.

But there are habits far more significant than just the way we speak or gesture. Many of our attitudes are no more than habits that we have learned through reinforcements. What religion do you practice? Was that a conscious choice or were you brought up with those particular beliefs? Do you practice religion? How about your attitude toward money? Has it always been there for you or do you watch every penny even though you might be pretty well off financially? Do you live in the city or the country? Where did all these preferences come from? The answer is usually habit. Someone taught you what kind of choices you should be making and, without questioning, you do believe and internalize those beliefs in most cases. They have become comfortable, routine and you are familiar with them. Other beliefs or practices probably even seem foreign to you.

The whole point of advertising is to create familiarity with a product or a name. The intent of most advertising is simply to get the name out there to such an extent that it becomes familiar to you. Repetition. Say something over and over, create familiarity, and eventually it becomes familiar and comfortable. At least you accept it as routine and normal because you've been exposed to it over and over to the point you internalize it. You now recognize it and it isn't foreign to you.

The ability to influence someone by creating name, or brand, recognition is a powerful tool. And you are the target of that influence every day whether you realize it or not. So you have to ask yourself, who or what is influencing your thoughts and perceptions. Who or what is affecting your habits?

This concept of familiarity was the basic idea of the "marketing" scheme of Nazi Germany before World War II. And it is the basis of most marketing techniques today. Repeat, repeat, repeat in simple, easily remembered slogans that have appeal emotionally to people on a broad level. Emphasize only the positives about your idea (or product) and do everything you can to present any opposition (other products or ideas) in a negative light. These were fundamental tenets of Adolph Hitler's propaganda minister's, Joseph Goebbels, program to create tremendous influence over the German people to support the Nazi party. That is not an indictment of the German people of the time as, I honestly believe, most really knew nothing of the atrocities that were committed. But the effect of the propaganda techniques were so powerful that the people trusted the Nazi party to such a high degree they didn't think to question anything that may have created doubt in their minds about what was happening.

Advertising works to influence you in ways in which you are not even aware. Why do you think businesses spend millions of dollars for seconds of ads during the Super Bowl? Because it works to sell stuff! No company would spend that kind of money for a short message if there wasn't a concrete financial return on that investment.

Here's something to try that may show you what I mean about brain patterns and how they can be programmed or even manipulated. Try this yourself first but in written form it may not work as well as if spoken. Definitely try it on a friend but verbally. I think you'll be surprised.

With a real sense of urgency repeat out loud as fast as you can the word "TEN." Say it over and over and faster and faster.

Really urgently. Quickly now, move onto the next page and read it out loud and follow the direction at the end.

URGENT!
QUICKLY!
HURRY!

SAY IT OVER AND OVER!

TEN TEN

TEN TEN TEN

TEN TEN TEN TEN

TEN TEN

TEN TEN TEN

TEN TEN TEN TEN

TEN!

Now, as fast as you can, answer the following question out loud **quickly**:

"WHAT'S AN ALUMINUM STOP SIGN MADE OF?"

QUICK ANSWER: ______________________________

What was your answer? If you answered “TIN” you are like most people I’ve done this with. Your mind sought the quickest route to a reasonable answer based on the closest pattern it found, “TIN” is pretty close to “TEN.” Of course the correct answer is “ALUMINUM” and the question even tells you the correct answer.

Repetition, habits, they are real and they can dictate your actions and thoughts and you may not be aware or even correct.

Your Habits

What I’d like you to do now is write down some of your habits and routines. Then ask yourself “why?” They can be just simple everyday things like which sock do you put on first? Do you have a cup of coffee 1st thing? What route do you take to work? The point is to examine what you do routinely and ask “why?” If you want to dig into “why” try asking that question five times for each habit. You may be surprised!

Once you’ve done that start to ask about some of your deeper habits such as why you vote or don’t vote. Why you like certain people and not others. Why you are or are not religious.

Question yourself in order to understand yourself – to “find” out who YOU really are. You will often find you don’t know why or you were taught by someone else. When you strip away all the stuff learned from “others” you might just get a glimpse of the real YOU!

Now try it. Use the following format or take a sheet of paper and just start jotting down your habits and routines. Then write down, to the best of your knowledge, why you do them. Be honest. This is one of the difficult exercises. Again, be honest but be aware.

For example, what side of the bed do you sleep on? Do you brush your teeth first or shower first? Do you read the news during breakfast? In what order do you dress? Do you take the same route to work? What's the first thing you do at work? Where do you have lunch? What do you have for lunch? Who do you talk with? What brand names do you consistently purchase? You get the picture: any routine at all. What do you do, even on the smallest, most unaware level, routinely?

Then ask yourself if these are conscious decisions of your own or are they the results of somebody else's influence over you? Why are these your habits? Do you know how they started or who they came from? Do they even make sense?

You might find that you don't know why you do these things or how they started. They might not even make sense today but they may have once before.

Try ten or twelve simple things, nothing too complex. The point is just to make you aware that you likely do things you're not even aware of. Once you've written them and thought about them please consider how much you may be or have been influenced by others without your knowledge. Are these habits really what you want to be doing?

What would happen if you changed at least a few of these habits? Would you make a change for the better or do these habits work for you? In other words, are these things you would do today if you had to make a decision on your own?

Ok, on the next page just start writing and see what you come up with. You might be surprised!

A FEW OF YOUR HABITS	WHY? WHERE DID IT COME FROM?
1	
2	
3	
4	
5	
6	
7	
8	
9	
10	
11	
12	

Mind Muscles

How did you do? I hope you started to dig into yourself to find, or at least get some glimpse of the real you. If you didn't I would suggest you weren't digging deep enough. Remember, this can be hard stuff and will take time. Give yourself that time.

Now that you've written some of your habits and explored them, ask yourself whether you made a conscious decision to do each one. Was it really yours or someone else's choice? Are you doing it to satisfy somebody else's expectations or is it really your choice?

When we recognize that we live with so many preset habits, and we come to understand that we often don't know why we do things, and, on top of that, realize the fact that our perceptions can, and often are, wrong, we can start to see ourselves and the world around us differently.

Are we living by our own rules and our own conscious habits or are we simply repeating things that were somebody else's way of doing things? Are we trying to please someone else? And that someone else might be several generations prior to you even entering this world. So, with so much influence from others leading up to each of us, we have a lot to deal with.

Some examples:

- Why do men wear ties?
- Why do women wear high heels?
- Why do we drive on the right side of the road while other societies drive on the left?
- Why does the color red mean stop and green means go?
- Why do some people prefer cats and others prefer dogs?

- Why does the fork go on the left?

The big question: Why are some people pleased with their lives and others are not?

These are mostly a bit silly but think about it. We do all kinds of things based on somebody else's decision. In fact, they become so instilled in us we almost can't imagine doing or believing anything other. (Please don't try driving on the wrong side of the road though, ok?)

I had a friend who was cutting his lawn one day and he asked himself "why." He hated cutting the lawn, weeding, fertilizing, and all the time it took. He hated it! When he asked himself why then was he doing it he realized it was an expectation of someone else that he have a nice appearing lawn. His father kept the lawn nice and his neighbors all had nice lawns. He was doing something he really hated because he was taught that it was expected. He believed that in his mind. And he perceived that his neighbors expected it. In other words, he was doing all that crappy work for someone else and not for himself.

What did he do once he realized this? He contacted a landscaping company and had a beautiful rock garden built to completely replace his lawn. He broke his habit once he realized he wasn't doing all that work for himself. And his neighbors thought it looked great.

On the other hand, I have a neighbor who built a detailed model sailing ship. I mean detailed! It took him 18 months to build it and he sold it for $1,200. He was doing something he so enjoyed that the money and time didn't matter at all. He was totally lost in the project. Why? He was satisfying himself! He didn't do all that work and detail for anyone other than himself.

See what I mean? Again, the point is to understand yourself. Make your own decisions consciously and follow those things, create habits that reflect those decisions; those things that are truly YOU. Do things for yourself. (Really though – no driving on the wrong side!)

Easy to say, huh? Hard to discover if you've spent your life building habits and doing things for the benefit of others. So the question becomes "how" to change your habits once you've discovered some things about YOU.

And here is how. Build your mind muscles. In other words, develop new habits and routines that work for you; not for someone else. And you can do this consciously by becoming aware. This is a huge key to change and meaningful success and happiness.

Think of it this way: You're going to enter some sort of competition; maybe a 5k run or a bike tour. You don't just go out unprepared, right? You build up to it – or die during it! You practice. You exercise. You build your muscles and your stamina. Or you're going to really suck and it will be painful if you don't prepare. I know from experience!

My first bike tour. One hundred twenty-six miles in two days. "Tour" sounded really nice. I like to ride a bike and I like to "tour." Bought a bike and went out. No need to train for a tour, right? Holy crap! These maniacs didn't stop anywhere to shop or have lunch or sight-see or have a glass of wine. They simply rode their bikes. Over a mountain too! And the second day of the ride it poured rain. I was wearing sweats. They are great at absorbing and holding about 10 pounds of water. All the other "tourists" were wearing slinky spandex stuff.

I thought I was going to die! They told me there was a big party at the finish line and I did see a couple cars pulling away as I arrived – dead last! I have never been so exhausted in my life!

Misperception first on my part of what a bike tour really was. Then no preparation. Clueless. Totally unaware.

Then, a few years later I actually did a 200 mile ride and had energy to spare when I finished! I did practice rides up to 100 miles, ate properly, got the right gear, dropped over 20 pounds, and had fun! Awareness, knowledge, experience, training, preparation. You can do the same for your mind.

Start with some simple mental exercises. No, you don't have to check with your doctor first. You can do this now on your own! And no fees or insurance or memberships either!

Simple exercises include things like crossword puzzles or Sudoku puzzles. They can be simple memory games or puzzles of any kind. I am very sleepy and groggy in the mornings so I often start my day with a game of solitaire or a Sudoku puzzle. No, I don't always win but it does wake up my mind for the day.

Next try reading some; not too much unless you're really an avid reader. But even if you are, try reading something you wouldn't normally read. Usually something reflective or provocative will get your mind working. Read something that makes you think or question things. If you read morning prayers or the Bible for example, try reading something from another religion or other philosophy. The Tao is great for this, at least for me. Some of it is very inspiring and some I just don't get at all. But it makes me think and the passages are short. This is a simple mind exercise; not a competition, so try to keep it short. The purpose is to awaken your mind and give it some exercise. It's kind of like stretching out first thing in the morning or enjoying that wonderful stretch of a new day before you even get out of bed.

Do this long enough to allow it to become part of your new routine; a new habit. And be aware of it and why you are doing it.

OK, that's the light stuff. When you feel ready, move up to a new level. If you lift weights or jog or do anything, you don't start with the maximum. You start small and build. As you move on, and continue your mind development, try something a little more challenging. Try learning something new.

I suck at statistics! I consistently score in the bottom quartile. Is there a score even lower than that? I don't know. It took me four attempts to pass the second semester of statistics and finally get my undergraduate degree. Then I had to take it again for my MBA. What torture but I did pass (barely) with a C+. And I worked my butt off for it.

So a challenge for me is reading or trying to figure out a statistics problem. Yeah, mental torture. But it does expand (and expend) my brain and I find that every once in a while I actually "get it." Then it's an amazing feeling of accomplishment.

How about you? Try reading something way outside your comfort zone. Maybe try writing a letter or keeping a journal. Maybe just jot thoughts down throughout the day and assemble them into a calendar for next year. Maybe check out Toastmasters to learn speaking and presentation skills. Maybe take a class in something that interests you. Maybe just learn to balance your checkbook. Anything!

Just try something that challenges your brain and you will find that you will grow mentally over time. You will become more aware and better at coming up with creative ideas or solutions to problems that confront you. Solutions and mental resources you would not have had before. You won't be so automatic in responding to your perceptions or other peoples' wishes without thinking about them first. You will gain understanding and the ability to think for yourself. How great is that?

A World of Influence

What we've covered so far is all just to get you to consider that you live in a world surrounded by outside influences which may be real or may not be real. They may or may not be meaningful to you. But you might be preconditioned to respond in a way that really benefits someone else.

I hope I've influenced you so far in some way to begin to strengthen your awareness and your mind so you begin to think for yourself and come to better understand yourself.

That's right, even I am trying to influence you too, but in a way that benefits you.

I really believe we, together as a society of individuals who are each unique and contributing in some way to the overall good, can change the world for the better. I believe we have become complacent and way too comfortable. We rely on too many others to make our decisions for us. In the course of our lives, then, who is really finding happiness? Us or those others we are trying to please? Our individual uniqueness and strength of character built our great nation. We depended on ourselves and those around us for honest support. But we were all individuals.

Our parents, teachers, friends, and lots of other sources tell us who we are from the time we are born; at least who we are in their eyes. We are born totally dependent upon those around us and we grow up the same way too. Because we are dependent and also because we are social beings, we want to fit in and try to live up to the expectations of those around us; especially authority figures.

Now an authority figure for you may be the toughest kid on the block or some strict teacher. The question is: how do we know that they got it right? Remember, they are looking at us through their own individual perceptions and experiences of the world around them. They might be right. They might be assholes.

Only you can decide who you are. Yeah, you should listen to others but you've already spent most of your life listening to others tell you who you should be and how you should act and what you should say and on and on. Hold it a minute! This is what I'm asking you to question. How can you ever really find yourself or even begin to be yourself if you're trying so hard to be what somebody else thinks you should be? That's crazy!

I grew up with a father who didn't really get involved with me. He played catch once in a while and yelled a lot. He was already gone to work before I got up in the mornings and was out almost every evening at some meeting or other or playing cards with his buddies or just out for a drink.

My mother was living in La La Land where she imagined everything was very elegant and flowers grew year round. She had none of that life she imagined and was in total denial. But kept telling me how awful my father was and how wonderful I was. In her mind I was brilliant and physically strong. I was Young Mister Perfection. And I believed it! Of course I did. It was the only feedback I got. I believed it, that is, until I struggled in school and got punched in the mouth a couple of times.

Yeah, I was living and behaving according to the perception of myself that I got from my mother. I thought I was brilliant and better than everyone else. As a result I was never really good enough for anybody so I became pretty aloof. If things didn't go my way it was always someone else's fault. Combine this learned behavior with my natural inquisitiveness and you've got a first class brat, know-it-all, little asshole. Yeah, that seems like a pretty good description.

I was skipping church one Sunday by playing in piles of large boulders on a nearby hill. I found a spot I could actually crawl into, like a cave. So I pretended I was on some grand adventure and, best of all, I could see the church and when it let out so I could simply go home at an appropriate time and not be found out.

While on my adventure though two figures suddenly stood above me and blocked the sunlight. I couldn't see their faces and they were too big to crawl into my "cave." They decided to have some fun with me. I got peed on by a couple bigger kids from the really tough side of town and was actually grateful they didn't beat me up or stab me to death. End of my make believe adventure and I couldn't do a thing about it. Humiliated, I just went home.

Oh, and I sucked at baseball, football, track, and basketball. You name it and I was no good at it yet in my mind, I was a terrific kid. Right! A legend in my own mind. Oh, and my mother's too. Let's not forget that!

Even the church was playing with my head. That's another plus (not) for me: I was brought up Irish Catholic! I'm still recovering from that. But I do have to say that I did see so much hypocrisy and flat out contradiction that it did make me take notice of it all. Did you know you could actually buy time out of purgatory? Yeah. There was a chart in the back of our church that told how much each day your sentence was reduced for how much money. Jesus loves us but he also takes cash. I figured I had sinned enough to be ex communicated by the time I was about twelve so why bother even trying after that? Although I went on to Catholic high school I had to continue to play the role of a good Catholic boy. That's what I was best at, pretending to go along.

Yep, had my sights on college too. But nobody else in my family ever went to college so I never had a clue what I would actually study or do there. Oh, yeah, Ozzie and Harriet, the Lone Ranger, Superman, and many, many others gave me a view of what the world was supposed to be like too. All in all, I can safely say I was really screwed up and totally confused.

But where to turn to help me understand reality? I had nobody. Nobody until I met my wife and her family, that is. Yeah, up until then I knew what didn't work but I had no idea what did. And that's no way to live. That is not happiness or satisfaction or even contentment. I was well on my way to becoming an alcoholic and had just about given up until I met her. Something inside of me saw in her what could be and it was all good. I am a very lucky guy.

I still struggle almost every day, very much as I imagine a recovering alcoholic does. You don't just walk away from all you've been told and taught while growing up without emotional scars. But my life is really good and that's part of why I'm writing all this stuff. I want you to know just how screwed up it was for me and where I started out in order to encourage you to understand that you can eventually feel the good stuff in life and be happy too.

So, if you're still with me, read on! There is a way to get through all the weeds!

What are your thoughts right now? Take some time to simply pause and reflect.

PART THREE
LOOKING INSIDE YOURSELF

Now, Attitude

When you begin to exercise your mind you begin to think rationally for yourself. But we are humans and there is another aspect to how our minds work. It's attitude, or emotion.

Do we start our day happy and energetic or do we dread the coming day? Do we see the proverbial cup half full or half empty? Do we notice what's wrong more often than what's right? What kind of attitude do we carry with us?

Some of us seem to be naturally aggressive or bold. Some of us are born smiling and predisposed to being happy while others seem to be born just the opposite. The "nature" side of our makeup. But then there is the "nurturing" or "environment" side of us also. I think we develop something of an innate attitude toward things pretty much based on our experiences, especially when we are kids.

I mentioned early on that I grew up in a pretty dysfunctional home. I was afraid of my father, especially when he was drinking (often) and my mother was a basket case. A little side story here.

When I was very young my mother would bake cakes and pies and cookies from scratch. She would can fruits and vegetables, scrub the house, entertain friends, and do all the typical Mrs. Cleaver stuff expected in the late 1940's and early 1950's. (For those of you who don't know who Mrs. Cleaver was go online and search "Leave it to Beaver.") I was very young but I remember it clearly.

Throughout my mother's life she had a series of experiences and disappointments that actually made her a fragile person. She was the second youngest of a large family. Her younger sister, Mary Rose, died as a very young child, suddenly making my mother the youngest, the "baby" of the family.

Her parents were so afraid of losing another child that they gave my mother anything she wanted and catered to her every wish. Her older sisters complained that she got everything new while they mostly got all the hand me downs. My grandparents even drove her to and from school while her sisters and brother had to walk. Pretty special, huh? She became used to being treated like a princess.

Then along comes my dad. Dashing young man, popular, older, smooth talker, athletic. Oh, wavy black hair and tons of muscles too. Long story short, my older brother was an inconvenient surprise. Oh, the shame of it all in those days.

OK, so they got married and soon had another baby, a girl, whom they named after my mother's younger sister. They named her Rose Mary. But she was born with a defective heart and she died at age three, within a month of my birth. Now, I have three children and four grandchildren and I cannot imagine what it must be like to bury such a young child. But they did.

After that my mother focused solely on the tasks of the house. My Father worked, played cards, and drank. I think they tried to get on with their lives but whatever flame may have burned between them probably went out. They didn't talk much or share much between themselves. They kept busy in each their own way. My brother and I were pretty much left to ourselves and ignored.

Then, when I was three, my younger sister was born. The birth was extremely difficult, my mother almost bled to death, and my father was out drunk. My brother and I were shipped off to relative's houses for weeks. Of course, in those days we weren't told anything about anything. I had no idea what was happening or why. At that age I didn't even realize my mother was pregnant.

When I did come home there was a new baby and my mother spent most of her time in bed. And my Father was out with the boys. For my mother, no more baking. No more canning. No more anything. The house became filthy and the laundry piled up. I either played by myself in the attic with my brother's old toys or I played make believe games by myself in the back yard. My environment became one of solitude and darkness. The blinds were usually closed, my mother in bed. My father who knows where. My big brother at school or off somewhere. Me, a three year old now going on four left alone to find my own way each day. Baffled and curious about why all the changes suddenly but not old enough to understand or even to know how to ask.

Oh, there was a little boy next door and my mother would make me go outside to play with him. Of course, with almost no parental interaction, my young social skills weren't really developing (at all). I really wanted a friend so I did go next door to play with Rickie. My opening encounter with Rickie was playing in his dirt driveway with metal toy trucks and shovels. Within about ten minutes Rickie decided to hit me in the mouth with a shovel. Split my lip and chipped a tooth. Rickie, I'm still pissed off.

So what does a four year old do? He runs home crying to mommy. Mommy's response? "Go back outside and play with him." Then she added one of her many gems: "The bigger they are the harder they fall." What? Are you crazy? He is bigger than me, he's armed (albeit a shovel), he's mean, and he doesn't particularly like me. Are you suggesting I should go and have a fight with him? Even at four I wasn't interested in getting my teeth knocked out. Then another of my mother's wonderful gems of advice: "Kill them with kindness." Wonderful advice! But I had to go out to play, and I did, but not to Rickie's house.

So what do you think my early childhood attitude was? Independence (left to my own devices for almost everything) and suspicion (people cannot be trusted). I'm not stupid after all and that's what I learned. For me, that was natural and I never thought to question it. Heck I wasn't even aware that I had an attitude.

So what about you? What experiences have you had, lessons learned, that have made you who you are today? Are you a positive person? Negative? Easily angered? Passive? Responsible? What? What do other people say about you? How would those who know you best describe you? Then, how would you describe yourself?

Seriously, think about it. Like before, give yourself some real quiet time to reflect. Try to write it down. What kind of person are you? How do you see yourself and how do others see you? Why do you see the world or other people or situations as you do? Why? Try again to understand yourself, the real YOU as you are.

Spend some time on this. Look back on your experiences and how you reacted. Think about how you approach situations. Your attitude toward things is kind of like your style. You may have become aware of your surroundings; become aware of what you do, your habits, and you may have opened your thinking capacity. But attitude is the way in which you see and move through the world, your natural "style" if you will. Think about it. A lot.

Use the following page to write down your life story. Use more paper if you need to. Tell your story about your family situation. What was it like growing up? What were your parents like? Your siblings? What events helped shape you from the earliest times you can remember or even some of the situations into which you were born? The earliest events probably have the most unconscious impacts but there are probably some events during your teen years too that impact you to this day. Try to remember the sounds, the smells, the sights around you and how you were treated.

Put a "plus" after those positive experiences and a "minus" after the not so pleasant ones. Also write how they may have impacted you at the time and what they may have taught you. These are likely the things that shaped you into how you see the world today. They may have reinforced your natural inclinations toward happiness or they may have caused you to question those around you. How did those early events impact you? Please remember that most of these things you really had no control over. You really made no conscious decisions about these things. They were just the way things were or things that just happened. You may not have even been aware until now but I believe all life situations and events have an impact in some way; especially in young children.

MY EARLY EXPERIENCES AND SITUATION:

SITUATION/EVENT	DESCRIBE YOUR REACTION – YOUR FEELINGS ABOUT IT	+/-

Now go ahead and use the next sheet on this page. Start by describing yourself in terms of your personality today. How do you react to situations? How are you with friends and loved ones? How do you act when confronted or frustrated? Do you spend time alone or do you prefer being with others?

THIS IS HOW I SEE MYSELF TODAY. THIS IS HOW I BEHAVE IN VARIOUS SITUATIONS. THESE ARE MY PERSONALITY TRAITS:

WHEN THIS HAPPENS	THIS IS HOW I TEND TO REACT – MY FEELINGS ABOUT IT	+/-

Now compare the last two sheets and try to find the links between your early experiences and your attitudes today. Like I said, use more paper if you need to.

Do you see any relationships between your early life events and the person you are today? Can you identify the positive impacts as well as the negatives? Very often you may learn how you got from being a little kid to becoming the adult you are now and what shaped you along the way.

Knock, Knock! Who's Really There?

By now you should be able to look at yourself with new eyes. You may be baffled by what you see. You may see yourself clearly. I don't know what you are seeing in yourself or how you are reacting, but you do. Regardless, my goal is that you now have the skills to sort out the real YOU and that you are becoming more aware of where you come from, what is around you, and why you are who you are in what you say and do and think. There's no judgment in any of this; just understanding and getting to know the real you. There's no shame. There's no guilt. There's no bravado. Just understanding.

This all takes time so please don't hurry. And keep practicing the previous exercises and continue thinking about the things I've presented to you. Keep notes too and look back on them from time to time. Remember, your ultimate success will be as you define it for yourself. This takes time.

OK? Ready to continue your journey? The next challenge now is that of being completely honest with yourself. Hopefully, you've done your best to be honest with yourself so far but there can be more to it when you look as deeply as I'm asking you to.

Most people, if they don't truly understand themselves, tend to rationalize their behavior, especially when they don't really know why they do what they do. It is simply too easy to tell yourself you are who you are because of someone else or some event beyond your control. You just do it. (No, that's not a NIKE subtle plug.)

But having used that phrase, "Just do it" does bring up an interesting point. Remember back when we talked about perceptions, advertising, and how you can be influenced by others? That's exactly what advertisers try to do. They literally do not want you to think.

I happened to be in a Nike outlet store recently and spotted a smiling young man wearing a T shirt that had "Believe the Hype" printed on it. I honestly thought it was a joke until I realized all the other employees were wearing shirts with the same message. They don't want you to even think about a product, including theirs. They simply want to create a perceived need in you. Then they want you to automatically react by predisposing you to buy their product. Sound weird? Maybe, but I believe it's true. They want a habit formed. They are literally training us in a manner very similar to how we would train a dog.

Create a need or stimulus (dog treat shown). Repeat your command (Sit) until the dog reacts the way you want. Elicit a behavior (Dog sits). Provide a reward (Give a treat). That's how it works.

How about this? Create a need or stimulus (Guys, you really have to drive a classy car to impress people.) Repeat your message over and over until you get a reaction (Yeah, I'll buy the shiny red one that I saw advertised on the TV (about a hundred times) and in the newspaper, and on the dealer reader board, and everywhere else.) Here are the keys and we'll throw in the fancy steering wheel (Oh boy, do I feel gooooood!)

Yeah, you feel really good until you have to pay for a repair, make that car payment, fix the dent, or maybe just have to wash the thing. Oh, and don't forget the cost of gas! They didn't repeat that part of the message over and over, did they?

So the question is whether you are satisfying your needs, wants, or desires or somebody else's. Is a flashy car really you? Or is it someone influencing you? Only you can answer that and only if you really know yourself.

We all have needs. Needs to be accepted, to be loved, to be able to be heard and appreciated. Influencers understand this and appeal to these needs. Marketers are masters of this and will use every technique possible to influence your decisions. But if they are influencing your decisions then those decisions aren't really yours at all, are they?

Before you can ever be successful, whatever that means to you, you must first understand yourself and know what your specific needs and wants really are. Then you can decide what is truly important and meaningful to you.

Then you have the keys to begin to achieve success.

What Do You Like?

I'd like you to take some time to think about some things that you really, really enjoyed or wanted to do since the time you were a kid and up until now. What have you done or still do that you really like or are so proud of? Go ahead and write them down. They may be silly things or just very simple things. Maybe it's camping or fishing or driving fast. I don't know. What pleases you?

These things are the positives in your life. Maybe you still enjoy them but maybe they've drifted off over the years. Too much to do at work. Too busy with the kids. Can't afford it. Or maybe it just seems silly now. But you liked these things and they may help bring you joy again. They help define the positive parts of your life. And maybe you're right: they were pleasurable once and not so much anymore. That's ok. But remember, even your history is part of who you are today.

So, use the blank area that follows and write down at least five of those positive, fun things you experienced in your life. Use more paper if you want to and write more than five if you want to.

Then write why they brought you pleasure. What in particular was it that brought you happiness or just a fond memory, or a smile? In other words, appreciate and understand them and you will come to know yourself better.

Go ahead. We'll wait until you're ready to go on.

MY HAPPY THINGS: ☺

WHAT WAS/IS IT?	HOW OR WHY DOES IT BRING YOU PLEASURE OR SATISFACTION?
1	
2	
3	
4	
5	

Next Up: What or Who Influences Your Life Today?

Once again, find some quiet place with some quiet time just for yourself. Get a cup of coffee or whatever you might like (no beer, wine or other "spirits" – you will want to be clear headed for this), and a pen or pencil. I'm giving you another worksheet to fill out and if you need more space grab some paper also. If you do need more space to write, please don't sit in front of a computer or tablet. I want you to have as little distraction or separation between you and your thoughts as possible. Just a page, paper, pen or pencil, and your handwriting. Just you. The old fashioned way.

Start by only writing your name on the top of the page or sheet of paper. Simple enough?

Now write down some of the things that influence you or have influenced you today. It might be your present situation or something that you experienced or learned years ago that you are very aware of and carry with you almost every day. This book might be one thing. Maybe your job. Your spouse. Your parents. Your siblings. A teacher. Advertising. How about a book you read or a special movie that affected you? Maybe the neighborhood where you grew up. A friend. Maybe some event in your life or a situation you had to work through. Might be something very positive, very negative, very neutral at the time, or some combination. Each life is different.

For me, it's my upbringing, the Catholic Church, the Vietnam and Cold Wars, the "Bomb," the economy, my marriage, my children and grandchildren, my career, friends, and more. You get the idea. Now write at least 10 things on the next page. Don't worry about the extra column. We'll get to that shortly.

Go! I'll wait again. Let me know when you're done, ok?

This is where there would be soothing music and lovely scenes of fields of grass or forests or a bubbling stream. All stuff to help you get in touch with yourself.

How's this?

THINGS THAT INFLUENCE ME TODAY

WHAT ARE THEY?	(WE'LL COME BACK TO THIS COLUMN)

Done?

Ok, so now write down in the right hand column how they affect you. What impact do those things have on you; especially your views of the world or other people? Most importantly, how do those things make you who you are and how you behave or what you believe to be true?

More music, more coffee, some other relaxing, enjoyable and soothing beverage (other than you know what). Really give this your time and your thoughts. Nobody else is going to ever read what you are recording so you can be totally honest. In fact, if you're not being totally honest you will know it and this will be a waste of time. Please don't waste your time. We only have so much in this life.

Go ahead now and write some more. Let me know when you're done. I'm having coffee so I'm in no hurry.

Well, how did you do? Yeah, you may have written stuff you already knew but maybe you discovered something too. Did you find anything that seems kind of dumb today that happened a long time ago? Did you find that you still hold on to things that are long gone and really don't make sense to hold on to any longer? If you did that's great!

Maybe you found nothing earth shattering and that's fine too. But I hope you gave yourself a picture or some insight into some things that may be, or have, influenced you to be someone you aren't. Or, maybe you found that you are trying to please someone else. If you are holding onto something negative that is now long gone but still may influence you please ask yourself "why." Is this still affecting you? Do you want it to? I call these things your "baggage." And it's ok to put it down and let go.

If you found some very positive influences you might want to hold these in some level of esteem. Why are they positives for you? What about them made a difference? I call these things building blocks and you can use them to support yourself when you need support. You can also share them to help others.

Your Storage Unit (Some Assembly Required)

It would be very unfair of me at this point if I didn't talk about how to deal with what you may have found in the previous exercises. If you were really honest you may have uncovered some pretty difficult things that you may or may not have been aware even existed in your mind or were influencing you. I don't want to leave you hanging in any way but I do want you to be aware at this point. And I know this might be the most difficult part of this whole journey.

So let's start with the baggage you may be carrying.

If you found someone or something that is or has influenced you in some negative way you may have known that before you ever started the exercise. Maybe you got some new awareness and maybe some very bad old memories came to the surface. Bad things do leave scars in our minds and sometimes even physical damage that remind us daily that we have suffered. From my own life and those of loved ones and friends I could offer many horrible examples. But I won't burden you with those. You have your own.

It's really easy to say something stupid like "Just let go and move on." But you and I both know just how stupid a statement that really is. Especially with the scars or other damage you carry either physically, emotionally, or both. Yeah, maybe it is kind of minor stuff but maybe there is some pretty heavy stuff too. What to do?

First, if you really have some serious stuff going on that continues to influence you it can be like a rock holding you under water. You're not free to move around as you wish and it's even almost impossible to breathe. If you really can't let go or escape that please seek professional help. That alone might be difficult to admit but there are professionals out there who can help a lot more than this book can. Please go see someone professionally trained. That may be someone in your religion or it may be a PhD type or a medical professional. I don't want you stuck with that rock tied to you.

I know it is hard to admit to certain life situations and the way they may have affected you. Been there and did have to go get help myself. It doesn't make things go away but it does put the past into perspective. I do believe your past is always a part of you and it will influence you but it doesn't have to be a negative influence.

So you decide you have some baggage but not serious enough to seek professional help. You're a self-help kind of person. Ok. So what do you do? The answer: dig it up, confront it, be aware, make it positive, and put it away. Well, that's easy, huh? No.

Doing the previous exercises can dig it up and help you be aware of what really happened and how it affects you today or made you go in some life direction because of it. In some way it affected you.

A lot of people seem to stop right there and hold on to the negative experience to the point it defines them. These people are seldom happy in any way in my opinion. In fact, they seem to want to share their misery and, instead of growing out of their bad experiences, they want others to come down to join them. You've met them. Always looking at the down side of things. You see them coming and can almost see that dark cloud hanging over them. You hope they just keep walking and dread having them stop to chat with you. Sorry to say this, but does that describe you sometimes? If it does, you're carrying your baggage with you every day and you've probably become so used to it that it seems natural to you.

I've known several people who carry their baggage like that and want the world to know how heavy their burden is. Gotta tell ya, people don't want to hear it. I've also seen some baggage carriers who are so used to carrying that burden they refuse to put it down. It is too much a part of them. It totally defines them. Others, though, simply don't know how to put it down. Letting go starts with being aware that it is a burden. To actually put it down requires almost extraordinary strength and a real desire to change; to change who you are and recreate yourself. It's scary. And it's not easy. I know from personal experience on my own part and having worked with others.

But I also know it can be done but it usually requires some help from someone else as well as an internal willingness to let go of the baggage and find yourself again. If you're carrying those bags please be aware you will likely need a really good reason to want to put them down. What is your reason, if you want to let go?

A word on why you want to let go: I've learned that doing something for the sake of someone else is great in the short term but doesn't work long term. If you want a change, it must be for yourself. If you quit smoking for the sake of your family you will struggle and likely not succeed in the long run. If you put down whatever that baggage is for the sake of someone else, the same applies. You may do it for a while but, in the long run, you will likely fall back. Not always, but the odds are not in your favor.

Some positive and successful techniques I've used or have seen work for others are these:

First and foremost is the need to be aware of what it is that you would like to change. Then, understanding why you want to make that change. It may benefit someone else but it must be for your betterment first. You are doing this for you.

Develop a positive mental image of the change before you even start. If you are intending to stop some behavior or give some up, don't think of it in those terms. What are you gaining by no longer behaving that way or doing that thing you want to change. It's really hard to stop or give up something. It is much easier to imagine and keep in mind what you are gaining. It also helps to imagine that you have already succeeded. There's an expression I've heard several times and I don't know where it comes from. "Fake it 'til you make it!" Act and think as though you have already accomplished your goal. Sure, it's totally bogus at the beginning but it puts you in a frame of mind that eventually makes you comfortable with that particular achievement. It does work so give it a try.

As an example, I quit smoking years ago. It took two attempts and I really had to psych up for it. The first shot was one of giving up cigarettes and cigars and stopping for my health and for the benefit of my family. It was able to struggle through it for almost a year until a friend and his wife had a baby. We had cigars to celebrate and the next day I was smoking again. I could only hold out so long and I actually did pretty well but I never really saw myself as a nonsmoker.

A few years later I came at it with a different approach. Yeah, I psyched up again but this time I imagined that I was a nonsmoker from the beginning. Even on the first day I mentally told myself that, yeah, I used to smoke, but that was some time ago. It was only hours but I kept repeating this to myself. Then it became days and I kept repeating that I used to smoke but that was in the past. Eventually, my mind came to believe it somewhere in my subconscious and I no longer had any desire to smoke. The mental struggle was gone and to this day (more than 45 years later) I think of myself in the same way: Yes, I used to be a smoker but that was a long time ago. I could smoke again but I have no desire to even try a cigarette.

Plan for the change. After heavy lifting for a long time, it isn't a natural thing to just let go. Prepare for the change. You can do that by imaging how your life will be different. Imagine being free of that baggage. Visualize it. Think it. Smell it. Don't deny it but begin to see it as something in the past. Being in the past, yes, you experienced it but it is in the past and there is probably nothing or not much you can do to change it now.

Pretend in your mind that the change has already happened. When you're ready, put one of the bags down. Gently. Just one piece of baggage. After a while you can put down some more but you know nothing lasting happens overnight.

A lot of this book is about goal setting and identifying steps to attain those goals. Prepare for this as you would for any other goal. Some of this book also deals with habits. Carrying baggage is certainly a habit that has been reinforced in some way over a long period of time so it will probably take some time to change the habit too. Be ready for that.

Beyond your planning and preparation, there are basically two aspects about baggage. One, you can do something about it or, two, there is really nothing you can do to change it.

If you find there is something you can do about it then consider doing it. What might that be and what are the consequences? Think it through well before you actually do it. Maybe confronting someone. Maybe making some reparation or an apology. I have no idea what it may be specifically for you but give that some thought. If you can change a negative past then do so when you are ready. Be prepared though for push back if you do confront and try to change the past. And it might hurt you all over again. If the risk of that is too high you might not want to go that route and realize that you cannot really make a change. But if that does happen you can also become aware that it was you who tried to correct the past – you. In that knowledge you can start to see it in a positive light and be free of it. I'm not suggesting it goes away but I am saying you can live better with the knowledge that you at least tried to make it different. That's a plus.

If there really is nothing you can do about your baggage you can symbolically let go in a few different ways. You can write down what happened and how it affected you. You can add your thoughts about it all and your desire to let it go. Then burn it!

You can write a letter to someone who affected your life and explain how you feel and mail it to them. If that someone is no longer available you can write it and put it away in a box or burn that too.

You can bury the letter or notes somewhere. Journals can help. You can talk about it with someone you trust. Get it out of your mind in some form like writing or talking. It's like breathing out, a big sigh.

Best of all, you can use those building blocks I mentioned earlier and, in your mind, create a box using those blocks. Mentally put the negative or hurtful influences inside that box and put it away. Yeah, it is there and you know it but it is contained and separate from the rest of you now.

Finally, search for ways those negatives helped you in some way. Negatives give you understanding and can build strength and character. Maybe you learned some valuable lesson from it that you can pass along to others.

The Vietnam War caused the Air Force to move me to Montana first, then on to fairly dangerous flight missions overseas later. And being who I am, I hated the structure as well as having to be away from my family so much. There was a lot of negative influence in all that for me. But when I think about it, it also paid for much of my education, gave me discipline which I really needed, and forced me out of what would have been a mundane life stuck in the past. Through effort over time I was able to replace my bitterness about the whole thing to realizing the good that came out of it all.

Finally, forgive. Forgive those who may have hurt you. In my entire life I have only met a couple people I would truly identify as "evil." Most people are victims of their own experiences and really only want to be recognized and appreciated. They may have hurt you or negatively influenced you in some way but, at least I like to believe, they were just being who they were, the result of their own life experiences without being aware or able to do things better, unlike you.

One Plus One Equals You

I told you this was not going to be a "follow these 7 steps to success and happiness." This is a lengthy process and by now I'm guessing I've lost more of my readers who actually thought I was joking when I said this would be hard work. And we're only getting started.

If you decide to press on then good for you. If you think this is too much, ok, maybe another time. I wish you the best. Really.

So now you are an aware individual person who has begun to understand that we are born into circumstances over which we really have no control, we are influenced by others from the moment we are born (and maybe even from the moment we are conceived), and we grow up being told over and over who we should be. But you have begun to understand that and you have taken a first look at the real you. You've gotten a glimpse into what you really like or enjoy and you've begun to identify what influences you and to question those influences.

Not bad at all. Give yourself a star.

So, Who Are You?

Take a look at what you've written so far. How does it feel? Does it make sense? Do you see any patterns in your life? Like before, the whole point is simply to begin to become aware of who you really are. After all, how can you be successful or happy if you're trying to be someone you're not?

So the question is: Who are you? Hopefully, you now have some better picture and clearer insights into the remarkable and unique you.

And Where Are You Going?

When businesses start up one of the first things they do (or should do) is write a business plan that tells all about the business, the why's and how's and expectations. It serves as a guide to activity and, ultimately, to the success of the business.

An important use of a good business plan is that it can be handed to someone (like an investor or even an employee) and it tells the reader all about the business so it can be assessed objectively. The writing of a business plan is also important for the owner because it forces him or her or them to deal with reality and be objective about the whole business.

For several years I taught Small Business seminars under a Small Business Administration program at a local college. Whenever I taught business planning most of my students would have what they considered fabulous ideas for a business. But when they got down into the details they would typically find it wasn't really quite as fabulous as they originally thought.

One very nice individual knitted socks for cats and intended to open a store in the mall expecting she would make a wonderful living doing this. Uh, maybe not. But better to understand that mall store rent would far exceed her cat sock income potential before she went out and bought too much yarn, right?

Well, that's kind of what I'm trying to get across here. Better to know who you are. Better yet, what is driving you to do things? If you had to tell someone who you are and what you believe in what would you say? Think about it.

And now, write it down. No, you don't have to show it to anyone but if you do happen to have a really close, trusted friend, you might want to have that person take a look and see if it rings true. This would really have to be a great friend or partner!

As an example, here are some of my own "who am I" answers. (Yes, I trust you but not with everything about me.)

- I'm prone to compulsive behavior.
- I struggle with staying focused on one thing at a time.
- I value family unity and support.
- I value total honesty and directness. (This is probably why I also tend to piss people off.)
- I believe in working for what I receive.
- I value humor. I love to have a good laugh.
- I like to help others succeed.
- I'm lousy at sales.
- I really like dogs. (Maybe because they don't need socks?)
- I have to stay busy.

How's that?

I could write a lot more but how about you? Please take some time to write down your description of you. (You have noticed by now that I also like to write things down – makes it real when you have to put it into words rather than just think it.)

Use this space and add some more paper if you want to.

THIS IS HOW I DESCRIBE "ME"

Now the big question becomes this: Are you living according to who you really are?

I just want to point out that we haven't begun to address how to become successful yet, have we? We are laying groundwork that will point you in the right direction and I think that is one of the most important things you can do for yourself and others. First, know yourself. Then, go out into the world and do your thing to the best of your ability. That's what's coming up in the rest of this book.

PART FOUR
Doing Something (Successfully)

So far we've talked about perceptions, influencers, trying to discover who the real you is. That's great but we haven't actually done crap, nada, nothin', squat. Right? So are you up for using what you now know and actually doing something? It is so easy to day dream and wonder and imagine stuff in your head but, if you're going to live your life you have to get up and actually go do something. Sorry, but it's true.

And maybe you are doing stuff. But is it the right stuff for you? Ah ha! That's the question now! And believe me, I know how to avoid, how to procrastinate, how to let others do it, and how to pretend I'm involved. In fact, I'm a master at it.

And that's exactly what drives me to push myself into weird situations in which I have to be totally visible and accountable and challenged all the time. But at least I've learned this about myself and it helps keep me in balance (along with my practical spouse's insights).

Back to my family and growing up (still a work in progress). Remember I mentioned my father picked me up by the throat and how my mother dropped out of life? Yeah. And all the tension that would take another book just to begin to describe.

But then remember also that I mentioned my father wasn't really a bad guy after all?

Well, here's the deal. Since my father couldn't stand my mother's prissiness, and he honestly liked to hang out with other people and party, he actually was doing what he believed in. He was having as much fun as he could in his life and he was being active in all kinds of things.

Why then didn't it all work out at home? Because my mother could not forgive him for having wronged her. In fact, he forced her unconsciously to confront the reality that she wasn't a fairy princess. She was his wife and the mother of his children. She couldn't confront him. She simply didn't have the skills or the fortitude. She was totally unprepared to deal with him on any level. She, and all the rest of us, were afraid of him but mostly because she taught us to be; to cower and avoid him at all costs. Like an effective advertising campaign, she told us over and over how awful a man he was.

On the other hand, when I was older and married with my own children, he came to visit us not too long before he died. The monster I knew was just a little old man in frail health. But he still liked to party and tell jokes, drink a few beers, and tell fascinating stories. He hadn't really changed at all I realized. It was then that my wise wife asked me what I thought he wanted out of life. I thought about it and realized he just wanted to enjoy life with his family. My mother blocked every avenue open to his happiness that she possibly could. I realized he was simply not a bad man after all. (Forever grateful to my wonderful wife!) He was simply frustrated! Totally!!

He was lacking in one important area, however. He had no skills whatsoever in dealing with my mother. Was it an unfortunate situation and marriage? Yeah. Was it hurtful?

Yeah. Did he try to make it better? Yeah. Did my mother try to make it better? I'm sorry, but I have to say no to that.

So what's the lesson here? Unless you choose to become a hermit you have to learn to compromise with people, yeah, even yourself sometimes. You can't have it all all the time. The world just doesn't work that way. On the other hand, it cannot just be you working at something that involves others. Other people have to work at it too. That's a big lesson to learn.

So, what is it you would like to do or to accomplish or to change in your life? I certainly don't have a clue unless you give me a call and we talk about it but my number's not in this book. (You can contact me through my web site or e-mail though.) I guess that means that you have to decide. I can help with that.

Look back now on who the real you is and what were those things you really enjoyed or do enjoy now. You might have some burning desire and that may be why you bought this book in the first place. Or maybe you're just not content and aren't really sure what you want in your life. OK, I get it either way. So, you know me, let's make a list.

To start, make it an easy one so you are more likely to get a hit, a success. I really wouldn't recommend something like ending world hunger, or making more money than Bill Gates. Not bad targets but that is shooting a little higher than reasonable, especially for your first time out. Don't worry, you can end hunger and make more than Bill Gates later. For now just ask yourself what are some simple, not too hard, things you want to accomplish or change or do? Write them for yourself and then pick the one that really resonates with you; one that does matter (but, remember, not too hard – have to walk before you run, right?).

Use the next page to list those possible goals and achievements you may have in mind; things you would enjoy but haven't done or things you used to do that you've let go of. Remember, as you write them, keep them achievable. The simpler the better. Use the headings to help you identify which might be the best choice for you by scoring a few factors for each idea.

Use a scale of 1, 3, or 5 for each factor and score your idea. A "1" is the lowest score for a factor. You would give a one, for instance, if the idea is very hard to accomplish, takes a long time to achieve, is very expensive, is not really practical, etc. Get the picture? When you're finished scoring add up the scores and the highest two ideas should get your attention to seriously think about and consider. Try for at least five things but more if you want to.

Ok, once again, spend some time on this. And, again, I'll have another cup of coffee. See you again on the other side.

IDEA	EASE	TIME	COST	VIABLE	OTHER	TOTAL SCORE
1						
2						
3						
4						
5						
6						
7						
8						
9						
10						

Now really focus on the top scoring one or two things. What would it be like if you achieved either of them? Really, how would it feel, look, sound, taste, what would people say, what would you think about having achieved each one? Go ahead, and savor it as if you've already done or accomplished it. Dwell on that for a bit.

Now before you go too far, would there be unintended consequences that might outweigh that accomplishment of either? For example, maybe you've decided that you really want to prance around the office naked on your next birthday. Cool! And it might be fun. Just sayin'. No judgment on my part. Hmmmm. Might that make future work difficult, or maybe impossible? Yeah, you might really want to do it but, ah, maybe not a good idea. There's a social compromise that may be necessary here, right? And if you're willing to really be yourself and go for it, then go for it. (I can't believe I just gave that advice! I wonder what my consequences for that will be.)

Back to your selection (having noted the possible consequences). Have you picked one? Good. Now what are you going to do about it? Why haven't you already done it? What's been holding you back? Those are all good questions to ask yourself because you might have a really good reason for not having done it. But if you don't, I gotta tell you that you're spinning your wheels. Let's get you out of "stuck" mode and get you moving toward a fuller, richer, more enjoyable life.

Where to start the activity toward actually doing something? Somewhere along the line somebody taught me (and I've used this most of my life and taught it to many others) to start by simply stating your goal on the top of a piece of paper. Oh, now would be a good time to talk about goals in general so let's do that before we go further.

Setting Goals

Goals, according to good business practices, and I've found it true most of the time, should be "SMART." Well, duh, why would you want to write a "DUMB" goal? On the other hand, some will teach that goals should be "Big Hairy and Bodacious." I have no idea what a "DUMB" goal is but I do know what the other two are.

The "Big Hairy Bodacious" goals are those you really stretch for sometimes. They aren't necessarily achievable or even realistic but they inspire us toward a greater vision. Kennedy's goal of putting a man on the moon and returning him safely is an example. It motivated our country to action and, eventually, success. Who knows? You might just succeed.

A "SMART" goal should be Specific, Measurable, Achievable, Realistic, and Timed. Isn't that clever? To be honest I'm not entirely clear on the difference between "Achievable" and "Realistic" but what the heck; it really sounds great.

But eventually, the "Big Hairy Bodacious" goal has to be translated into a "SMART" goal to actually get it done.

When I lost my job while living in Montana I figured out what my minimum income requirement would have to be as I searched for work in my then career. I searched throughout the country with this number in my mind and, lo and behold, guess what I got paid at my next job? That's right, the exact minimum I had set out for myself. That set me back at least ten years financially. The lesson I learned was to never aim too low. Be reasonable, know your minimum, but aim high. Why not? If you miss your high target at least you're not at the bottom of your barrel.

I can't wait to get to the section about dealing with difficulties. That will clearly include my boss from hell who fired me. Ha, Ha, Ha. Before I get too maniacal about it, she was awful but I actually have come to appreciate the experience for all I learned. She was a perfect example of going after self-serving goals without regard for either others involved or consequences. Needless to say, we didn't really hit it off. But I owe her a certain amount of thanks.

So, what about you? What I recommend is writing 4 or 5 only of the top things on your mind that you would like to do, fix, change, achieve, whatever. If nothing pops into your mind right away, think about something simple or look back to that list of what you enjoyed doing but aren't doing any more for some reason now. Think about what you've wondered about. Remember, this is about finding yourself and it's about action – doing things.

What about taking a class in something that used to interest you? What about that little something that nags at you but you never quite get around to? What about just improving your gas mileage? Anything. Just keep it simple. Like everything else, build a foundation of experience and you create a solid foundation.

Got 4 or 5 things? Good. If you haven't already selected one previously, now is the time to pick the one that seems both most important and most doable. One might just jump out at you but in case it doesn't, try this: Like the earlier exercise, pick a criteria by which to compare them to each other. The criteria might be "Easy to Do," "Time to Do," "Cost to Do," "Significance or Impact." You might pick some others. Then put a value on each criteria. You can use a system of 1, 2, or 3, or 1 to 5, or just use 1, 3, or 5 to keep them spread apart. A 1 is the least value and the higher the number the higher the value. You can actually begin to quantify your thoughts this way and it helps make decisions easier. I do this a lot and it does help although I don't always agree with the results. There is a qualitative side to things too. You shouldn't forget that or you can become a robot.

Then simply score the items you picked and go with the one with the highest score or, if it doesn't "feel" right, don't. But ask yourself why and understand what's driving you to override the score just so you are aware and you understand your decision.

It might look like this:

POSSIBLE GOAL	EASE	IMPACT	TIME	COST	NOTE	SCORE
Take a Statistics Class	2	3	3	3	To improve myself	11
Take Golf Lessons	4	2	3	4	To have more fun playing	13
Take Spouse out more often	4	4	5	3	To enrich our marriage	16
Lose 10 pounds	2	5	5	5	To Improve my health	17
Read a Biography	5	1	2	5	To gain insights	13

Notice that the more favorable the factor, the higher the score. Take "COST" for example. The lower the cost the more favorable that would be so the higher the value assigned. Makes sense?

So for me my highest scored possible goal would be to lose 10 pounds as it scored a 17. Notice that I value taking my Spouse out almost the same as I value my health. So, recognizing that, I have to think about it a little and I agree. Spending time with my Spouse is very important to me and to our marriage. So, understanding that, and giving it a lot of thought, I've decided that if I don't lose weight I won't be around or healthy enough to do things with my Spouse. So one kind of drives the other. And, I think I can do both. Now, I'm strongly recommending you pick ONE only. But there are times when one or two go together and are so related it makes sense to do more than one.

Do you see that this is quantified subjectivity? I know that makes no sense but we are complex humans. We have minds capable of building computers but we also have emotions. Quite a mix, huh? It means nothing is really simple, ever.

But I can focus on losing those ten pounds so that I can be healthier and more active in doing things with my Spouse. There are many other benefits but for now I'll stick with the one goal and also focus on the single benefit that I enjoy.

Now do a gut check with your goal. Does it resonate with you? Is it something that you can trace all the way back to one of your very basic motivators? No, maybe not dramatically so but is it consistent with who you really are? If not, you better think about either the goal you picked or your basic desires and values.

Picking a goal and actually getting on with it with it are two very different things. Achieving that goal (the whole point of this book) is coming up next!

Notice something else. What happened to the concept of "SMART" goals? I think, now that you have some actions to consider, this is a really good time to take another look at your goal. Is it really smart? Let's put mine to a test.

Is it Specific? Yes. I targeted to lose 10 pounds. That's something I can measure and is very specific. It's not "I'll lose weight," or "I'll trim down." Ten pounds is very specific. Passed!

Is it Measurable? Yes again. Due to how specific this goal is, it is also measurable. Passed again!

Is it Achievable? Yes it is. It's not so much weight that it would make it so difficult that it would never happen. If I weighed 350 pounds and shot for dropping 10 pounds that would be very achievable. However if I weighed 110 pounds and went for 10 pounds that may be a different matter. In my case I think I can do this realistically but it will be a bit of a push for me. Maybe I should consider dropping 5 pounds the more I think about it. I want this to clearly be achievable. Ok, so ten is a little bit of a stretch and a stretch goal is ok too. Stretch goals though tend to be more long term in nature. So I think I'll change my goal to 5 pounds with a stretch goal of 10.

So now my goal has changed because of the SMART test. Now it is:

My New Goal: Lose 5 Pounds

Continuing on with the SMART test:

Is it Realistic? Yes on this one. Given my life style, my habits, my awareness of my weight, and my desire to do more and be healthier, this is a very realistic goal. So this one passes.

Is it Timed? Oops. No, it's not. Losing even a specific amount of weight passes all the other tests now but I didn't put any kind of time on it. It could be really easy to put it off until tomorrow as they say. I could have all the right reasons to go after this goal but if I don't put a time measure of some sort on it I may just keep putting it off. Setting a time also helps establish some accountability and an ability to monitor progress. For instance, if I set out to lose five pounds it could be a pound a month or even a pound a year. That can be ok. Setting a time schedule of a pound a day may be a bit extreme but on the other end setting a pound a year, ah, a little too lax maybe?

So, again, what's a realistic and reasonable time measure for your goal? Remember, it too has to be SMART. But now you have at least two specific measures that you can track, chart, report to yourself (or someone else if you wish), but more importantly you will know exactly when you have reached your goal! Hurray!

For me, I think I'll give myself 3 weeks to lose those five pounds. I'm looking ahead on my calendar and see that there are several dinner parties coming up and a holiday picnic. That would make it difficult to lose the weight. I could give myself a week if I really worked at it but I want this to be achievable and an extra couple weeks will insure that I can get this done. This isn't something urgent and I will want to lose some more as a longer term goal so why rush it?

Keep your own situation in mind and make this first goal easy on yourself. Too much pressure will make it all the more difficult. The old Japanese proverb says that "a journey of a thousand miles begins under your feet." You probably heard that it starts with the first step but check it out. It doesn't say that. What I take it to mean is you plan where you are going before you ever even take that first step. Taking steps without knowing where you are going is called wandering aimlessly. Spend some time thinking and planning.

How are you doing? If you've gotten this far you're doing great. Not too many people give the kind of concentration and consideration to what they do and where they are going that you are right now. And not too many people really succeed. Too many seem to just muddle through and get by. And all it takes is a little time, a lot of thought, and some good planning and the world can be yours.

Back to work! (Sorry, but I told you this was no seven steps to euphoric success!) Stick with me if this is starting to come together. Leave now though if you're still not convinced. Please don't waste your time. It is so short and so precious a gift and it is the only one that is given equally in that we all have 24 hours in a day. How we use it and with what skills makes all the difference. And we don't really have any idea how many of those 24 hour days we have, do we? Use them wisely.

Your Personal List of Possible Actions

Now you've got a reasonable goal I hope. Not too difficult (baby steps), it passes the SMART test, and you have possible action items. Just having a goal doesn't really do anything. You have to have some sort of action plan toward the actual accomplishment of that goal. So now it's time to look at your long list of possible action items.

Write that goal (that you fully understand and that fits into your life and your desires) on the top of the page that follows. Like before, if you need more space take a sheet of paper to continue. (No, I'm not getting any royalties from any paper companies.) Find that quiet place you like so much. And now let 'er rip! Yeah! Start quickly writing everything that comes to mind that you could possibly do to achieve or at least move forward toward that goal.

Anything! Don't think about it. Don't edit. Don't get too lengthy. This is a situation where "just do it" really works. It does help to do some sort of creative exercise first like I mentioned earlier in this book just to get your creative juices flowing. This should be a fun part with no holds barred. Free for all thinking. Blurting it out as quickly as you can. Go for it!

Here's an example:

My Goal: Lose 10 Pounds

- Exercise every day
- Eat less
- Eat more nutritious food

- Cut off my toes
- Get a liposuction procedure
- Go hiking
- Go bike riding
- Join a health club
- Remove a kidney
- See a doctor
- Join Weight Watchers

And on and on. You get the picture. Try to write at least thirty possibilities. And expect that you will run out of ideas around 10 or 12. Stick it out and a few more will suddenly pop into your mind. Note that some are ridiculous. Some ideas are just dumb but I didn't rule them out or even think about judging them in any way. Not yet anyway.

OK, start blurting out ways to achieve your goal on the next page:

MY GOAL____

30 WAYS TO DO IT:

1	16
2	17
3	18
4	19
5	20
6	21
7	22
8	23
9	24
10	25
11	26
12	27
13	28
14	29
15	30

Any More?

By making such a list you started using your creative juices. I appreciate how hard that is for some people but I hope you did your best. Again, this is all about you and your life; your world. When you come up with a bunch of ideas even though they might be really out there and not practical at all, something else tends to happen inside your brain. It seems that subconsciously you start to mentally work on your goal and you will likely find that you start coming up with possible action ideas out of the blue. That's your subconscious working. You might start to notice things related to your goal or one of your action items; something you never noticed before or thought of before. I can't tell you how many times this has happened to me. Your brain is a magnificent efficient living machine.

In other words, your total resources can start to focus on your issue or your goal even when you're not thinking about it. To me that's just incredible and wonderful! So use those new thoughts. Read over your list and add to it as new thoughts pop up. I really think you'll be surprised how this works and, ultimately, how it becomes a help in actually achieving that goal or solving that problem.

As you look over your list of possible actions pick out three, four, or maybe five that will have the greatest impact toward achieving your goal. Don't discard the others but concentrate on those that seem to you to be most doable and will give you the best results. You can again use a number scale and criteria by which to score your better ideas or you can also use the SMART test to see which really are best. Don't fall into the trap of picking the ones you think you "should" do. Pick the ones that you really can do.

Sticking with the weight loss examples I could have a possible idea of not eating any snacks. Yeah, that would sure score high but I like snacks and I get hungry between meals. I could probably do without for about three days then I would really struggle to not eat a bag of M&Ms. I would probably damage myself with this one more than help myself in the long run so it's probably not the best idea compared to some others. So, for me, it might be better to allow myself a light snack or even a few M&Ms during the day. Get the point? I'm not saying some action steps won't be difficult but don't pick ones that are so difficult for you personally that you are actually sabotaging your efforts at achieving that goal.

Once you have picked a few, and just a few, action items you actually have to do them. Oh Gee! Yeah, this can start to get hard.

Goal setting is a relative thing. For example, if you happen to be very over weight or want some really significant change in your life, it would probably be more of a challenge than me losing ten pounds. Oops, that's five pounds now!

I teach baby steps and long term thinking instead of short term, quick fixes. I want successes to be permanent and sustainable. If you're looking for a really big change you probably have developed habits that are significantly ingrained into your behavior. You will not magically transform yourself overnight by shear will power. To change long held, strong habits will require more work than if you only have small, lightly practiced habits. So to go for a big, challenging goal you have to start with something very small. If it's weight loss on a significant level, maybe just skip a bite; just one. Then when that becomes a habit, build on it and just skip two. Or maybe park your car one space farther from your door each week. Habits build on habits and over time things do accumulate.

Savings accounts are like that. I remember when I was a kid of about 10, I sold flowers I picked from a nearby field. They were really just weeds but they were very pretty and people paid me for bunches and bouquets of them. And I started a savings account. I became a saver. By the time I was sixteen and had a paper route for a few years too, I always had several hundred dollars in cash in my room and my savings account was almost $1,000. To me, it all meant a sense of freedom and I didn't have to rely on my family for anything anymore; not that I could count on them anyway. I had become independent and my own person by then, as I am to this day.

And I started with $.25 that soon became $5, then $10, then $50. I was delirious when I hit $100, then $200! The other kids never seemed to have more than $5 or $10. Saving was my habit and my reward was that I never needed to rely on anyone. Not the best motivation but then I was never taught to rely on anyone and I became almost totally self-sufficient. Today, I have learned to give, to share, to care and love others. But that sense of self sufficiency remains, although modified so much, and it has become my tool to help others become free of their baggage if they are willing.

Small steps. Long term perspective. Slight improvements along the way. And, frankly, a little help now and then too.

Your Action Plan Detail

By now you have refined your goal and decided upon several feasible, doable action steps. Looks good on paper, doesn't it? Haven't actually done anything yet though. This is still preparation and thought to prepare your mind rather than just jumping in and doing anything. Although there can be a place for quick, obvious actions too, the types of things that are really so easy they don't require much thought. For the long term success though, some thought and planning is required.

Now you have to convert your thoughts and ideas into an actionable and measurable plan. And a good plan details the execution of the action idea. In other words you have to know what steps to take to achieve the action idea, how they will be done, and when. That's a plan of action.

Suppose your goal involves a step that says you will save the money to do whatever. Great. How much? How often? When will you have the money you need? How will you get the money if you're not saving now? Do you even have a savings account or some other way of accumulating the money you need to achieve your goal?

A plan is a lot like a schedule of events that leads up to some conclusion. You should be able to put the steps of your action plan idea onto a calendar and actually track your progress. And do think of it as progress toward your ultimate goal.

Let's say, you need $1000 to go get that thing you have decided you really want. Break that step down to its parts. Yeah, another list for each of your ideas. More work. More planning. But, once again, this process will ingrain in your mind your creative concept of achieving your ultimate goal and you will find that the more detail you put into it, the more your subconscious will work on it, and the more reinforcement your mind will create. You start the flywheel turning and it gets easier and easier as you go. You'll see if you stick to this.

You may decide to get that $1000 a bit at a time. How? Well, maybe you can only cut back on something else, like a cup of coffee and save a couple dollars a day. Physically take the two dollars and put it aside. By doing as many physical activities as possible you are seeing tangible, reinforcing rewards start to accumulate on your journey to $1000. Those kinds of reinforcements keep you going forward and the more you can come up with the better.

Now, you can measure your progress toward the idea of "save $1,000." Yeah it's only $10 the first week but then it's $20. This is going to take a while, isn't it? You are progressing but you start to think this is ridiculous. This is going to take almost two years! That's right. But, how long would it take to achieve this goal that you decided upon if you didn't save anything? Yeah, forever versus two years.

But your mind is working if you keep at it and suddenly you find another way to save an extra $.50 a day. Not a big deal but look what's happening. You're now at $2.50 a day. Say it took you a month to come up with the idea for the extra $.50. So you have $40 put aside from your coffee savings when you start saving $2.50 a day. Now you are saving at the rate of about $50 a month rather than $40. The two year wait just became about 19 months. Better. And you keep at it as you remain focused and thinking about it. Your plan details evolve and just keep getting better if you keep at it.

The point is to get into the details, get it on paper, get going, and stay at it. You will succeed eventually.

Something else may happen too. You might decide you don't really want to wait that long to get $1,000 and you may decide to change your goal to something that requires a little less. You're still going after what you decided upon but came to realize that you don't really need that much to satisfy your goal. On the other hand you might come to realize you really need $1,200. Well, that's up to you, isn't it?

Remember the point I just made above: details, action, stick with it and success or achievement will follow.

PART FIVE
KEEPING TRACK OF IT ALL

"Great works are performed not by strength, but by perseverance." - Samuel Johnson

In the course of writing this book, I heard a school principal today speak to a young group of middle school aged children. The school year ends for them tomorrow and they were recognizing outstanding performers from among the classes. (One of my Grandchildren received recognition for his efforts in language arts! Oh, yeah!) The principal commented that there are things we just are not good at but we have to learn to work at those things all the harder than those things that come easily to us. He called it "perseverance," and equated that ability to the ability to achieve success.

I agree.

Your life is a whole series of events. You have control over some and you have no control over others. It's important to recognize that fact. But it should not stop you from persevering, from pushing forward, from expanding your boundaries and growing. It should not hinder you in setting your goals or deciding your own personal future.

By now you have at least some sort of a goal and plans for that goal. So how do you keep it alive and moving? Again, perseverance! That's another thing that's easy to say but not at all easy to do. So the next question is how to keep it all moving toward your goal.

A couple of things to help you: First, remember "small steps?" Yeah. Those are really easily reached milestones you can follow so you will see that you are progressing. Each accomplishment, each milestone, is a reminder that you are going forward and each of those accomplishments should be celebrated in some way.

The second thing is to measure your progress in meaningful ways so you know when you reach that milestone and deserve a reward. What you are doing is changing or reinforcing new behaviors when you give yourself positive rewards one after another as you move along your journey.

An example: I really want to take a trip to Ireland next year. I haven't planned this one out in detail yet so I need to do that first. It starts with my wife and I talking about why, when, how, all that stuff. I don't know how much it costs either. So my first steps are pretty much investigative. It's really easy to say "Let's take a trip to Ireland next year." It's much harder to know exactly where to go, what month is best, how do we get around, and how much will we have to save to achieve this goal, which, by the way, doesn't even meet the criteria of a real goal yet. It's also really easy to just keep talking about it without actually doing anything about it. That's called an "idea." Clearly, it is not a goal.

So my wife and I have to start identifying exactly why Ireland and not France or Italy, or should we be working on some other idea such as saving up for something else entirely, like a new car or an improvement to our home? Let's assume this trip becomes the priority and we select it as our actual goal with planned details. Heck, even the planning of it can be considered a goal in itself that requires the SMART test and time lines or milestones.

We will go through our process and create milestones to mark our progress. Let's say we have the following steps agreed to:

- Talk with friends who have gone to Ireland
- Contact a travel agent
- Plan a time to go
- Cost out travel and tourist options
- Plan our itinerary
- Book our trip
- Go and have fun

These are pretty broad step to follow but they do constitute a general plan. Of course, each will have details attached to it. We can then put a deadline date on each general action and check it off when completed. If we miss our deadline we will know we are off course and jeopardize our ability to take the trip when we want.

Another milestone will be around the costs. We will have to put aside a fixed amount of money periodically in order to meet our financial goal. This one is easily tracked. You can even graph these things and keep track of them that way. In business this is known as a Balanced Score Card. You track your progress against your primary goals and objectives. Like this:

GOAL: Trip to Ireland for 10 days in one year in July.

OBJECTIVES: Investigate family history, see the sights, have fun.

STEPS AND PLAN:

TALK WITH FRIENDS WHO HAVE GONE TO IRELAND:

- Identify who we know who has gone by end of this month
- Contact each of them by the second week of the next month
- Visit with each friend and learn from their insights by end of next month

CONTACT A TRAVEL AGENT:

- Identify at least 3 likely travel agents by the end of this week
- Visit their offices by the end of the following week & gather information

And on it goes. Yes, it's definitely ok to revise your plan as you learn more about your goal or even about yourself. No, it's definitely not ok to just put it all aside and forget about it unless you really have a powerful reason. If you allow yourself to just put things aside, I'm sorry, but you will not succeed. You must push on to succeed. You must do the hard work. You must persevere.

Take a look at the travel plan that is evolving in the example. We now have specific dates and quantities. Once we determine costs we will also have a budget to follow and track. Say, for instance, we determine we need $6,000 for the trip. We have a full year until we plan to travel. That means we need to put aside $500 a month. If that's not reasonable then you either have to brainstorm how to get additional money or you will have to put off your plan or lower the cost. You cannot get there by hoping it all works out.

A word about credit is appropriate here. If you don't have the $500 a month and you plan to finance the trip with somebody else's money, you will actually be paying more than the $500 a month when you end up paying that somebody (the credit card company) back because they charge interest – compound interest usually. I hate owing money as it only digs you into a hole deeper and deeper as time goes on. Yeah, it's certainly ok for an emergency if you absolutely must pay for something.

Here's a thought and some advice though: Pay yourself first. Have you ever heard that before? It's really true. If you put aside only $10 a month for yourself you will have $120 at the end of twelve months. If all goes well it will be $240 at the end of the second year and so on. I am not adding interest because the savings institutions hardly pay anything in interest so if you do get a couple of extra bucks from the bank all the better.

More on budgets later. The point here is that your plan to accomplish your goal is now measurable and you can put dates and numbers on your calendar or on a tally sheet or a spreadsheet. And you will know whether you are on track or not. It's no different from a map showing you the way.

Set your milestones along the way and be sure to celebrate as you reach each one. You decide how you will celebrate. If you are working on saving money I wouldn't suggest you go out and spend a bunch but do something you enjoy as a way of celebrating. I would suggest a special picnic or maybe a hike or maybe just spending a few dollars (just a few) and going to a movie with your spouse. Anything that supports your goal and helps reinforce your actions, your new habits, as you progress ultimately toward achieving your goal.

A final word on tracking your progress: Pick a set time and place to review and document your progress. Maybe it's every

Saturday morning over a cup of coffee in the kitchen. Maybe it's on your front porch once a month at 5pm just before or maybe just after dinner. Whatever. Just be consistent. Treat it as an appointment with yourself. And don't be late!

Try sharing your progress or posting it up on the mirror where you can see it. Keep it in front of you and find ways to hold yourself accountable. My wife and I have certain financial goals so she gets a report from me twice a month and we discuss our budget and our financial plans. No surprises, shared understanding of our goals and our progress, and no arguing about money!

And it holds me accountable. Her too for spending our money conservatively. It only makes sense to have your spouse or partner totally involved in anything that you both have a stake in. It is so much easier to discuss issues intelligently and reach agreement on issues that affect us both when we communicate up front and early on. To be honest, sometimes I forget this and it bites me eventually.

PART SIX
FAILING CAN BE A GOOD THING

Somewhere I heard somebody say that only those who aren't doing things don't make mistakes. I used to be considered a very successful manager with very creative business ideas that ultimately became big successes. What I didn't tell people is that I actually averaged about seven total flops for each even moderate success. My CEO once told me he would like to put a statue of me in the lobby. Boy was I flattered until he told me why. Not because I was so successful but because I simply tried things. To his great credit, he was the one who created an atmosphere in which it was ok to try and fail, at least on a small scale. He was a great leader.

Most business ventures do fail. Little kids fall down a lot. What do they have in common? They try. They usually fail. They keep trying. They get better. They learn what works for them. They learn what doesn't work. They press on.

Some kids will learn to run at Olympic speeds. Some businesses become wild successes. Most don't. Sorry, but that's just a reality. You can spend your life as a wannabe or you can get on with real stuff. Your choice. If you listen to all the markcting crap out there and don't make those conscious decisions of your own you will end up falling short in the long run. Do you look like a Victoria Secrets model? Do you think you should play golf as well as Tiger Woods? Advertising would have you think you should if only you buy their product(s). RESIST!!!

Think for yourself and decide your own goals; not somebody else's. How many shirts have been sold with Tommy Hilfiger's name on them? I don't own any and why would I wear a shirt with somebody else's name on it? The idea of wearing somebody else's clothes just blows me away! I've never even met Tommy Hilfiger, he never calls me; we don't go out together. Why would I wear a shirt with his name on it? On top of that, why would I pay extra for it?

So what happens when you do come up lacking (according to the general "expectations")? You feel like you just aren't equal. Maybe worse, not good enough at all. Gee, though, if you only buy that one more thing…, then all will be well. Oh, until the next ad comes on that is showing how you don't quite measure up against the next product? Think advertising doesn't work on our subconscious and make us want and then buy things we wouldn't have even thought of? If you think that, consider why a minute of television or even Internet ad placements cost so much. Businesses don't spend money without a positive return.

I propose that it's ok to be a flop, a failure, missing the mark, whatever you want to call it. Huh? And you thought this was all about success, didn't you? Ha Ha Ha Ha! (In an evil deviant tone.) Well, actually it is. But success defined by you; not some talking head on the tube. YOU!

So failure of any kind by someone else's standard simply doesn't count. Rule it out. Totally disregard it. Advertising can be great if you find it informative or even entertaining. Some is really clever and hilarious, but not to be taken seriously. Remember, be aware and know thyself.

The other great thing about failure is that it teaches us things about ourselves. We learn what we're good at and what we suck at. We learn what things we really need to focus on and work at. Failure builds character and insights. I'm an advocate of good management principles which include Lean Six Sigma techniques. Don't worry, you won't get any lecture on that (at least not in business terms and there definitely won't be any statistics – have I mentioned I totally suck at that?) nor a test.

Yeah, you have to give things time and effort. If you fail first time out and give up you've probably given up too soon. Try to recognize why you are failing and work on those things. That's positive feedback and more valuable than you may appreciate until you come to understand and be open minded about it. Now if you keep at it and it's just not going anywhere that may be a different story.

If you keep trying and keep failing first look closely at why you are failing. Isolate those factors that are causing your failure. If you cannot control those factors or find ways around them or change your approach to obtain a different outcome, then I suggest you move on to some other goal. You've hit a boundary. Why continue to waste your time on this any longer? There are other things now you are free to pursue.

I think it is interesting to note here that many organizations have a tendency to promote individuals who excel in their current positions until they are promoted to a position that is way beyond their skill level. This is called the "Peter Principle" and assumes that if somebody is good at one thing they will also be good at another. Promotions continue until failure is achieved. Those organizations fail to realize that people can be valuable right where they are.

We are all different. Imagine a world in which we were all at the same skill level in every way, in everything. That's a nightmare for science fiction material.

Failure, after real effort, helps you define your boundaries. Everybody has them, everybody. No matter how good you are at something, someone else will be better. On the other hand, no matter how bad you are at something, someone else will be worse. This applies to your total life situation too.

So, "don't worry, be happy" sings Bobby McFerrin. You do fit in and you can make improvements. Just don't expect to be "the best" at everything or even good at everything. But don't let that stop you from trying. I love to play guitar and to golf. I really suck at both. In fact, I've damaged the nerves in one of my arms, my dominant hand, and cannot hope to ever play either well ever again. Doesn't mean I can't still get enjoyment. But you won't find me on the pro golf circuit or appearing at your local club this Saturday.

You don't have to be the best. It is up to you to carry yourself as far as you wish to go. Like paying yourself first, enjoy yourself first too. If you aren't full of enjoyment, how can you expect to share joy with others? How can you ever help others succeed if you don't find fulfillment yourself too?

One last short story here on this topic. My oldest grandson plays football for a small high school that happens to be in a league with some pretty big schools. In other words, his team is typically the underdog and gets beat most Friday nights, pretty badly. No, it's not fun. But I have to say that he and his team have developed a will to persevere. They simply don't give up and yet the odds are so much against them. They play hard, a lot harder than their opponents. They are learning strength of character and teamwork despite some overwhelming odds. I admire them at every game.

In their futures, when the chips are down, these kids will know how to keep at it. What about the other kids?

What about you?

PART SEVEN
Dealing With Crap!

This seems like a good time to talk about crap. It exists and you know it. Too many advisors and books and seminars about self-improvement, to me anyway, are full of crap. Oh, I didn't mean to say that exactly. They're full of really good stuff and I've learned so much from them, really. But very few talk about the dangers of the world or the negativity that we all know exists. We see it every day and I don't think it should be ignored. If you do ignore it, it can suck the life out of you and derail your progress and just pull you down. Want some examples? I'm sure you have a bunch but here are some of the things I've encountered:

Naysayers – focused on what's wrong or what may go wrong.

Gossipers – spreading negatives like a hydro seeder.

Co-workers who don't pull their weight but take credit for yours – sweet! (They may become your boss.)

Crappy bosses – a whole category by themselves.

Lousy drivers – drive you nuts and they usually don't have a clue.

Bills – especially those unexpected ones just when you were getting ahead.

Relatives – those who expect you to visit them but never come to see you.

Ex-spouses – says it all.

Serious illnesses – Yeah, they do happen to us or our loved ones.

Service employees who don't understand the concept of "customer" – Phony smile (when you finally hunt one down to help you).

How many pages of this do you want? We both could go on for many, many more, couldn't we? The fact remains, however, no matter how much we recognize the crap, what do we do about it? Usually, nothing worthwhile.

And so the stink lingers.

I guess I see all these things simply as obstacles to be dealt with. Kinda like weeds in the otherwise beautiful lawn. I do get pissed off but I have also learned to find these things entertaining. It can be like watching a comedy act because it is such bazaar behavior – slapstick. But if you are constantly subjected to it, it really can get to you. Wouldn't it be cool to have some sort of bubble surrounding you to protect you from all the crap? How about a containment bubble for the crap instead? Oh, yeah, and a toilet to get rid of it?

There are some techniques that can be applied to make those annoying things impact you much less. The first is to accept that crap happens. Remember the old bumper sticker that was popular for a while? “SHIT HAPPENS.” Brilliant message and so true. Sometimes you simply have to accept that it happens and there is nothing you can do about it except learn to get over it and avoid it spilling onto you.

The second big thing to understand is that when more than one person is involved in anything, yes, anything, there will be a problem or conflict of some sort sooner or later. It’s inevitable. Ask someone who has been married more than 50 years and you will likely get a response about how they learned to air their differences. But they do have differences and have learned to either tolerate them or learned to argue constructively.

I think Henry Ford is credited with the comment that “…if two people agree in business one of them is unnecessary.” I like that quote and have always tried to hire people with great skill but who are “different” than me. If you do that you surround yourself with a huge variety of talent. You do have to learn to orchestrate those talents and to become a referee at times. Above that, you have to be open minded and shut up and listen before making your decisions.

If you’re working on your own issues the same concept applies. Get as much differing information about your issue as you possibly can. Listen to different points of view before making the decision that you think is best for you.

Here are some tips I put together years ago after a consulting team worked in our organization to help improve morale and communications. In other words, teach everyone to listen and respect others while working together toward common goals.

DON'T EXPECT TO ACTUALLY LIKE EVERYONE: People are different but everyone has value. Look for that value and, unless it really rubs you the wrong way, try your best to tolerate those things that seem weird to you in others. You have to realize that if you don't like others, there are others who really don't like you either! If you keep this in mind it seems to keep you a bit humble and it also helps you remain open minded and learning more about others and about yourself. I see this as kind of a key to personal growth.

I had a boss whom I absolutely could not stand. I thought he was the most underhanded, negative, unsupportive idiot I ever reported to. He was evil! Yet so many other people in and out of the organization thought very highly of him; even others who reported to him. I couldn't understand it. I lost sleep over him. I avoided him every chance I had even to the point of not answering the phone when he would call me. I even kept a record of the horrible things he had done as I just knew he would either be arrested for gross mismanagement or he would fire me. Vinegar and water. Could not have been worse. It got so bad I was becoming physically ill because of our toxic relationship. But I needed the job and had to stick it out and just wait for him to retire (or me to have a stroke).

It went on like this for years until I got so sick of it that I decided to start just taking direction from him and quit doing all this damage to myself. After all, it's just a job and I had to stop letting it ruin my health and other relationships. And guess what? Our relationship began to improve. That didn't mean we became great friends or even liked each other all that much but I did begin to see just how smart this guy was and that his intentions were for the betterment of the organization. I started learning things from him and began to see things from his perspective. He was still very different from me, in fact, couldn't have a much different personality or style but by simply beginning to listen instead of avoiding, I began to learn and became better for it. Everybody, everybody, has something to offer regardless of whether you like a person or not. Everybody. (That includes you too in case you're feeling down.)

COMPLAINTS TO THE WRONG PERSON GET YOU NOWHERE FAST: Did you ever complain something like this: "I'm sick of them always trying to ____________________ (you fill in the blank)." And who do you say this to or who do you listen to when someone else complains in this manner? I'm guilty but at least I'm aware when I or someone else does it and I do my best to change it. As you read this and as I write this I'm wondering if you even see in the quote what the problem is. It's not that you're complaining. It's about how you are complaining.

When we use generalities in complaints we are fueling negativity and reinforcing or spreading gossip that really sounds appealing but lacks any real responsibility. Who are "they?" The other thing in that quote is the use of "always." It's an absolute. Really now? "Always," or its counter, "never." Those words in that kind of context are seldom true.

How does this sound? "Washington never gets it right. They always screw the little guy." It seems to be really easy to respond to something like this because it sounds plausible when we hear it. Then we get this general feeling that things are wrong. That then has a negative energy associated with our perceptions and before you know it you get this sense that everything in the world is against you in some way. It grows like mold in a dank dark room and our thoughts become more and more mush.

There's another thing that often happens too if you don't respond. Say you really don't agree with the person telling you this. So you stand politely and just listen then say to yourself, "Wow. That person is really off base." By being polite you're actually spreading the negativity. I don't suggest you be rude and tell the person to shut up because you want to surround yourself with positive thinking and positive energy that supports your progress and satisfaction. The naysayer would think you're nuts and start spreading stories about you!

By not responding, the naysayer can go to the next subject of the negative story and tell the next person that you were just talking about this same subject and that you agreed. No, you didn't but you might have done a couple "Ahh. Uh-Huh" comments. Now you're an accomplice to the negative perception. This happens a lot in work groups and even in social groups.

Do you know somebody who spreads negative crap like that and everyone knows it but it just goes on and on? Want to stop it? Here's how:

First, repeat back to the person word for word as best you can what the person just said. "So, you're saying Washington never gets it right. They always screw the little guy?" You might get a "yeah" response or you might start to get a clarification of some sort. "Well not always." The point here is that you have now challenged what the person has just said and only by simply saying it back to them. It can get them to hear what they just said and may prompt them to modify it when they hear it. It also tells them that you are listening to what they are saying and taking it seriously. You are beginning to hold them accountable for what they say and usually nobody does. If nothing else it can just get their attention.

If that doesn't work, simply react honestly to what was said. "Holy crap! The whole District of Columbia or the whole government absolutely gets nothing right? And the government always screws the little guy! Wow! That's a huge indictment of our entire government!" The person who told you this used absolutes when using words like "never," and "always." Another problem is the use here of "Washington." Do they mean the government, or a particular party or some office or what? What is this person really saying? But it seems so easy to say it and not be questioned, doesn't it? Once you react the person may clarify (or maybe just shut up).

Next, if you're able to, simply state facts back to the person. Maybe something like this: "Well, I'm a 'little guy' and the Veterans Affairs paid for my education and that of a lot of service people I know. That's just one example of many I'm aware of so our government doesn't 'always' get it wrong and 'screw' the little guy." Often, by stating facts rather than generalities you will find that the person starts to backtrack. The story then may change or even stop. Once again, you are holding others accountable for what they say and beginning to eliminate negatives that can eat your subconscious to pieces without you even being aware.

The final technique is to send the person off to talk to someone who can actually do something about what they are saying. When spreading negative comments they place a negative burden on you. Is this your problem in some way or is it theirs? Are you going to change what may be wrong with our government? How about when the person complains about taxes, or the boss, or a co-worker, or their kid's teacher, or whatever? If you're responsible for their complaint then by all means deal with it. Usually though, it's not your problem. If you want to help tell them to go see the person responsible for their issue. That means they have to deal with their problem; not you. And suddenly, you are free!

Try these a few times (they do take practice) and you will find those negative people will simply stop coming to you. Ah, sweet freedom! If you really like to gossip unproductively (that means waste time gossiping) then don't use these techniques. Your choice.

LIVE IN THE PRESENT. YOU CANNOT CHANGE YOUR PAST (OR ANYONE ELSE'S): I've done some really stupid and even some pretty bad things in my life that I'm not proud of and I'm not even going to tell you about them. I'm actually ashamed of some of them. And they haunt me to this day.

But I've done some pretty good things too that I'd be happy to share (another time ☺).

The point is that as you are working on whatever it might be that you define as your success or achievement, please don't define yourself by your failures or past experiences. Believe me, others will do their best to label you but you don't have to live by what others think. Yeah, if you are labeled it is something you probably do have to deal with but you can change things.

Think of it this way: When you were a kid and maybe homeless or even abandoned, did you have any control over your situation? Of course not, so why would you let something like that define who you are today. I admit those experiences are part of your history and do form your perspectives but if you begin to think for yourself and become objectively aware of all that is your history you can put it into perspective.

Remember, I grew up in a pretty strange family situation and I really had a hard time seeing it for what it was. Eventually, though, I was able to and that opened me up to explore a whole new world that suddenly became available to me. The past is called "baggage" but you are allowed to let it go and put it down. You don't have to carry it with you everywhere you go.

Think back to something dumb you did years ago. Do you still want to be held responsible for it? That was years ago and you were a different person then.

For the same reasons, do you still hold others responsible or label them for things they did in the past? If you do that's called a grudge and it will keep you from ever being able to see the value that the other person may offer. I'm not suggesting you go tip toeing through the tulips and just love the heck out of everybody. There are toxic people out there. Just stay open minded and look for those opportunities to bury hatchets.

BE SPECIFIC IN AS MANY THINGS AS POSSIBLE: A lot of this, I have to regretfully tell you, I learned from accountant types. Ugh! I hate having to be specific because then I have to have done my homework, done the research, and I have to present it accurately or I lose my credibility. Ugh again! But it's true. I even advised you to be very specific when setting your goals and action plans and again I advised you to challenge others who aren't specific. Maybe we should all be accountants! Ugh, ugh, ugh! Nah. I like to think of myself as "creative." How's that sound? Actually, the world, and success, requires both skills.

When you say something like "I'm buying a new car," people will hear different things. Some will think you said that you are on your way to the showroom and picking up the brand new, latest model wheels from the dealer. Others may think you only said you're getting a car that's new to you. Still others may think you said that you're planning to buy a new car someday.

What you may have actually meant was that your current car just broke down and you're upset and only meant you wish you could buy a better car. Wow, how many ways can you interpret what seems to be a very simple and clear statement?

What else do you say to others that could be taken the wrong way, misunderstood, and actually get you into some difficulty with the individual?

Here's an example of something I said and my son-in-law heard. He's very helpful and anxious to please others. I tend to speak in generalities or, you might call it, thinking out loud. We had just moved to the Puget Sound region, bought an older house that needed fixing up (another misleading phrase used frequently by real estate agents – the place was a wreck!). There was a wood storage … I don't even know what to call it … kind of a shed with an open front. More like a shelter in which to store firewood. The problem was that it was just ugly, poorly made, and had a lot of scrap stuff laying in it. It did serve a purpose though as we did need a place to store some outside stuff but protect it from the rain. There were many other things that needed to be done that were far more important than removing this eyesore and I had little time as I had just started a new job.

My mistake: I commented out loud in front of my son-in-law that I'd like to see that shed be gone. Of course, if it was gone I would have no place to store anything outside and I would also have to go to work immediately removing the scrap and replacing the shed with something else. Also, having just moved, besides not having time, I didn't have the money to replace it just then. Besides, there were so many other things that were far more pressing (like a leaky roof).

The very next day I came home from work and found that the shed had been destroyed. My son-in-law was very pleased that he had "helped" me fulfill my wish that the shed be taken down. It was. And I was now committed to work I could neither afford nor had the time for. He had done exactly what I had expressed that I wanted. Note what I had "expressed" was not entirely what I was thinking or intended. And it cost me time and money and opportunity to work on the more important things. He was really trying to be helpful and I appreciated that but…you get the picture. It was clearly my fault for not fully or accurately expressing myself.

And not just with others. Be specific with yourself too, especially when you are setting your goals and making your plans. If you need money for something, exactly how much do you need, by when, etc? The more specific you can be the more likely you are to understand your true progress and the better anybody who is helping you can understand clearly what you plan to accomplish. Instead of "plan" I almost said, "…what you hope to accomplish."

I recently heard someone say that hope is really only for those things over which you really have no control. I hope it doesn't rain. I hope someone calls. Hoping is just wishing for something so don't let yourself fall into the trap of hoping as it only tends to put off action on your part. No, you probably can't control the weather but you can allow for it by putting up an umbrella, can't you? Plan and act.

PRAISE OTHERS. BE KIND TO THEIR EGOS: You know, everybody has some sort of value if you look deeply enough. Sometimes you really have to dig. But more importantly, everybody wants to be valued and appreciated in some way. It feeds their egos and if you are the source of that ego feeding food you become more important and more valuable to them. So, why not? You can feel better about helping others feel good about themselves and, who knows, you might make a new friend.

Instead of fighting or disagreeing all the time, or avoiding others you don't particularly care for, try the positive approach. No, it doesn't mean you roll over and start to give false praise. Be real. There is some sort of value somewhere. Like my example of the really awful (in my eyes) boss. The only positive I could find when I started practicing this concept was that he was really good using a calculator. I've never seen anyone so fast and he was great with numbers (much to my chagrin). So I praised him for it. Like I said, why not? It did soften him if only for a moment. But it was a start that I was able to build on.

My wife and I were recently enjoying a night out and we stopped for a drink and to listen to a guitar player / singer. A small place and it was late. We were the only ones left in the place. The performer was awful. Wasn't playing anything all the way through, coughing and hacking into the mic, and playing guitar like he was trying to decide what to practice next. We wanted to finish our drink and just get out of there.

But, being the last in the place, it would have been embarrassing to just walk out on the guy. After all, this is his gig. So we thought desperately about what he was good at so we could at least say something positive on the way out. Ah, I liked the sound his guitar made when he used his slide! That's it! So I mentioned that on the way out and dropped a couple bucks into his tip jar. The guy came alive! He was so happy that he received a compliment – any compliment at all and he immediately started playing all slide guitar stuff. Turns out he was pretty good at that stuff. We did leave but the smile on that guy's face was every bit as enjoyable as listening to a great player. It just felt good.

EMBRACE DIFFERENCES OF OPINIONS: Imagine a world in which everybody is the same. They all look alike, think alike, are the same height, dress in the same style. (Let's keep the different sexes though, ok?)

If everyone thought the same and held the same opinions it would eliminate disagreements and maybe even end wars. That would be nice. But it would be a lot like a world of robots; almost like a science fiction movie (a bad one) and most certainly boring. A world without differences in people would likely only progress as far as you could progress personally and everyone, being the same, would be progressing on the same issues. In other words, we'd still be working on how to reach a little higher to get more paintings on the cave walls.

I read an interesting quote this morning. "We can complain that rose bushes have thorns or we can marvel that thorn bushes have roses." (Abraham Lincoln) That's a lot like the glass half full or half empty. We each see things at least a little differently than others. We are not all the same nor do we all hold the same opinions. That's our nature and to each individual, his or her own opinions make sense to them. Who knows? Maybe they're right or at least more right in their opinions than we are in ours. Maybe not but who is really to say?

Remember perceptions? Remember accepting what we are taught and holding on to those beliefs when, in fact, they may be wrong? Well, the same idea applies here in that we can expose ourselves to different ideas if only we listen and consider them for ourselves. Listen. Allow others to express their opinions. That means that you also embrace different perspectives and even just by listening, you surround yourself with different skills and values. It all serves to totally expand your world and your own views and gives you so many more options to consider when you are trying to come up with solutions to issues or just ideas to help you achieve your goals.

Embrace differences. Enhance your own understanding. Expand your possibilities. One size does not fit all.

Think about it a minute or two. Others have the right to express their opinions and to be wrong (☺ in our opinions) as long as they don't do damage to others. If you want to learn something, ask any 10 year old how to do something on your IPhone or your computer. You will be amazed!

IDENTIFY WHAT STRESSES YOU (AND OTHERS): My wife was on the verge of total exasperation with me last night. Although not that unusual given my personality (Thank you for staying with me all these years. I still don't completely understand what you see in me.) I was particularly pushing her buttons. We were both on edge with each other. Why? Because we both happened to be dealing with things that had nothing to do with each other or our relationship. But, being on edge with our own issues, we took out our own problems on each other. (That's real trust!) Fortunately, we know this about each other and recognize when we are doing this. But think about how many times you may be taking things out on others who have absolutely nothing to do with your issue. Or maybe you take it out on things.

Did you ever kick a wall or throw something or rip up something or whatever just out of frustration? How about yelling at the kids? Years ago in a place where I worked the managers would decide each month who was experiencing the most stress and we would send that person a stuffed toy dog. The idea was to acknowledge that person was under a lot of stress and it was ok to take it out on this company dog. I got it a few times and I don't think anyone ever actually kicked the dog but just knowing that others recognized your situation was a big help.

Stress is real in our lives. And in everyone else's too. I have an antique medical book from the early 1900's and it starts out mentioning these trying times and all the stresses of our modern world. Oh, to live at the beginning of the 20th century again! Stress has always been with us since before we came out of the trees and learned to walk on two legs and use our opposing thumbs. And it will likely always be with us until the end of our species. ("The end of our species: That's a stressful thought!) So we have to learn to deal with it.

Too much stress causes burn out. Not enough causes complacency. I guess that means there should be some sort of middle ground or balance of just enough to keep us moving without so much we melt down. So the question becomes how to keep it in balance.

The first thing is to learn to recognize stress. The next is to learn what we can do about it, if anything.

Sometimes we aren't even aware we are under stress until it is too late. I have learned over the years how to recognize my stressors but I don't know whether there is a standard way to do that for everyone. What I will suggest to you is that you use the next exercise page (yeah, again) and write those things you are aware of that do cause you stress. I've drawn a line down the middle of the page and want you to write those stressors on the left side. On the right side write what your behavior tends to be when you experience that stress. If you're not sure ask people around you. Believe me they will know.

Start by writing some basics like this:

STRESSOR	BEHAVIOR
Lack of sleep	Get frustrated easily – hard to concentrate
Hungry	Get anxious and irritable
Coming up on a work deadline	Start to criticize my boss & co-workers
Money problems	I ignore them thinking they will work out
My spouse is critical of me	I get angry and we fight

Now you do it starting on the next page. If you need more paper go ahead and grab some. Like always, give this some thought and some time. If you can't come up with anything you're probably either a saint, maybe a monk, or you might be fooling yourself. Everyone, even monks, live with some sort of stress.

Go ahead. Give it a try.

THINGS THAT CAUSE ME STRESS:

STRESSOR	BEHAVIOR

There's up to ten. Any more come to mind? Maybe later.

Now cover the Stressors on the left side so you only see the Behaviors showing on the right.

Start to consider the behavior first, as that is usually easier to recognize, and when you become aware of the behavior check to see if that stressor is causing it. Oh, yeah, you can add to the list as you go. Simple recognition of your behavior change is the beginning of dealing with stress. This can also work in recognizing that others are experiencing stress too.

Now that you have an inkling about recognizing that you are stressed (and often you are not aware unless you do a mental check or you have a really honest friend who will tell you that you are acting weird) what will you do about it?

Go back to the process of setting a goal that I so wonderfully expressed and explained earlier in this book. Let's take an example from the sample of my stressors and behaviors list above.

You recognize that you are becoming critical of your boss and/or co-workers (more than usual). And you stop to give it some thought and you realize that your workload has been increased for a special project. You feel you're being pushed to get more done with a time limit that might not be realistic. Ok. So what are you going to do? First, your reactionary behavior is probably not helpful, right? What positive actions can you take? Ah, make a list!! And then make a plan!

How about discussing the situation with your boss and/or co-workers? How about approaching the work in some different way? I can't tell you how you will deal with your stressors. The point is that you can deal with them and make things better for yourself if you recognize what is causing the stress and do what you can about it. I have found it amazing that just the act of recognizing what is causing me stress is about half the battle or even more and is such a freeing feeling. It allows me to focus on the real issue and not add to my burden.

Now there are things you don't have control over and it really helps to recognize those too. If some new regulation requires something, say a new speed limit is imposed and it now takes longer to get to work causing you to have to get up earlier and get your kids to day care earlier, there is probably not much you can realistically do about it. New taxes, new work regulations, weeds in the yard. Some things you will just have to learn to live with or do your best to accept in some way. Sorry. At least we aren't dealing with saber toothed tigers any longer. Cars and computers do stop running from time to time though with almost the same amount of danger as being chased by a tiger.

DEAL WITH REALITY FROM A POSITIVE POINT OF VIEW: Reality can be harsh. It can bite you in the butt. When it does it can hurt and it is really hard to stay positive. I think we all have a few bite marks. At least I know I do. So how do you stay positive?

You could say "I'm positive this really sucks," or "I'm positive I'm going to get fired," or whatever you want to be positively negative about. What good will it do? In fact, I've found you will start giving off negative vibes and people do pick up on that. Then what tends to happen is a self-fulfilling prophesy. When you think negatively your life turns negative. Gee, what a coincidence! I believe it was Henry Ford who said, "If you believe you can't, you're right. You can't."

You can lament your crappy situation all you want but it will do you absolutely no good. Been there a few times and nothing good ever came out of it. On the other hand, you can use your crappy situation to learn and avoid whatever caused that crap in the first place from ever happening again. No, it is not easy. Let me repeat: It is definitely NOT easy.

I got fired from a job (that I actually hated) by a terrible boss. I made a lot of money, had a nice house, and my kids were about to start college and one was planning on getting married. Being in a small town and having rather specialized job skills, I had no choice but to move. Where? When? How? Holy crap, what a mess!

This is one of the main stressors on a family; on a marriage. So this was a dangerous time and perhaps life changing in a very bad way had I or my family given up. These events can also be a source of great strength if you have a positive attitude.

I've heard a lot of people say that they don't, and shouldn't, share the crappy things in life with their children. It will upset them and scare them too much. Well, how else will they learn how to cope with the bad things that do happen if they have no experience or training? My wife and I have been through more than most people and we never excluded our children or kept them in the dark. I would think they, being children, would instinctively pick up that something was wrong with their parents' lives and that would frighten them more than knowing the truth. Of course, when talking with them and telling them things it must be appropriate to their ages. And, it must be in positive but realistic terms they can understand, right?

When I lost my job I came home, pretty upset and emotional, and told my wife first. Then, like every other night, we sat down as a family, had dinner, I bitched and moaned about my boss, and, guess what? My family was totally supportive, as always. Tough times were nothing new to us and we always pulled together.

My boss won the coveted "Asshole of the Year Award" that night and I got kinda drunk to celebrate. The next few days were spent figuring out what to do. And then we went to work on it. Everyone else in the family went about their business but they cleared out a room for me to set up a "job search" office. Then I went to work in my new office. Yep, kept regular working hours. Reality had already set in that I had to act and act quickly.

First, my severance wasn't all that great and I estimated I would run out of money before I could feasibly find a new position and relocate. So, scared to death, I called my (award winning) boss and negotiated a better severance than was originally offered. (By the way, I was forced to sign a "resignation" immediately upon notice of termination or there would be no severance at all – one of the many perks of being a mid-level manager!) Surprisingly, I got what I asked for! Had I not given it all some thought and began to deal with the situation immediately I would not have dealt with first things first. I could have languished in "hoping" things will work out.

Next I targeted certain areas, contacted all my friends and associates, and started by job hunt. I also continued to work out physically, take breaks, and end each day on my time schedule. My job was getting a job. There's a lot more to tell but I hope you get the point. What a lousy situation but I didn't let it get me into a negative state. Sure, there were days when I was scared and there were days when I was depressed and anxious. But I know that all situations are transient. Time passes and things do improve eventually if you keep at it. Having the support of others who care about you is helpful too but I believe that even if you don't have that, although a lot harder, you can count on yourself if you remain positive and deal with the reality of the situation.

Each evening, at supper when we all talked about our days, I would report my activity and any gains I made to the family. I was accountable and they were involved. We all stayed focused on lessons learned for the day and anything positive. We kept moving forward rather than lamenting a lousy situation.

By the way, all this did result in a new and better job in an area I absolutely love.

ACCEPT & ASSESS CRITICISM: You just might learn something about yourself. Listen first, talk later. That's all I have to say on this point. Just listen to what others are telling you and judge it honestly. They may be trying to help.

RECOGNIZE THAT OTHER PEOPLE'S PERCEPTIONS ARE REAL TO THEM: We learned earlier that our perceptions reinforce what we already believe to be true, even if it isn't. Well, recall that's true for other people too. As you grow to become more and more aware of your perceptions and learn to question them before totally accepting them (magicians will hate you) also realize that others may not be questioning their own perceptions, right or wrong.

If you become sensitive to appreciating that other peoples' perceptions are true to them you can start to understand what may make no sense to you at all when people open their mouths and you hear what they see through their eyes, through their perceptions of the world.

How many people stocked up for the end of the world during 1999? I don't know either but it was a big deal because people believed (based on their perceptions) that the world as we know it really was going to end. How about the Mayan prophesy of the end of the world? People believed the world was ending on a specific date and, despite the fact the popular date has come and gone (and we're still here) the debate and belief continues among many people.

How about just determining the value of a car? Perceptions vary widely.

I just sold a classic Ford Mustang for a lot less than I hoped (without reason) it would sell for; about 25% less. But, after all was said and done, it was a good price and fair. My perception was clouded with my emotions for the work I had done and the look of the car. To the buyer it was business.

Very different perceptions. So we met somewhere close to a realistic price that both of us were satisfied with.

One more caution here. If you assume you know what someone is thinking or what they believe, you will probably be wrong. No, I'm not going to say "You will make an 'ass' of 'u' and 'me.' Ha Ha Ha! I hate that saying. Way over used. So let's get it out of the way and be done with it.

People have perceptions of you, of themselves, of the world as they see it, just as you do. The only real difference is, if you've gotten this far in this book (Congratulations for sticking with it by the way.) and you've done your homework and given all this some time to sink in, you are aware that perceptions can be wrong and even influenced by friends, advertising, religion, your family, or any number of things you encounter.

I've been thinking about the Beatles recently and how they kept expanding their knowledge and experience with music from different cultures. Normally, you wouldn't want to listen to music from another culture but if you do for a while, you will start to hear a new musical language that can become a part of your total musical experience and enrich your appreciation overall. Expand you mind. Expand your knowledge. Expand yourself and you will be able to draw upon more experiences when you are searching for ways to solve problems or achieve your desires.

The World Is Ours

We live in such a diverse world and we usually only recognize a very small part of it. Look outside and recognize that others experience it differently and believe differently. As long as it is not harmful to others feel free to explore it.

I've often thought that the great curse or sin of mankind is that we actually are living in the Garden of Eden now. I've even wondered whether we are already living in heaven as most religions describe it. But why don't we see it? Because we have lost our sense of wonder and inquisitiveness. In other words, we already have it all but we don't recognize it for what it is.

This is our great misfortune until we come to understand that we live in an ever changing, moving universe full of wonders. And being sentient beings we could be seeking to understand as well as enjoy. Instead, our tendency is to isolate ourselves. That includes our way of thinking and seeing the world for the diversity it really holds.

Why not just listen to others and understand where their perspectives and opinions and thoughts are coming from? If you search by listening and respecting, rather than trying to prove your point, you might just find something new and worthwhile about your world through another person's eyes.

But, on the other hand, maybe not. At least be respectful and listen. Then take what you will from it.

PART EIGHT

"COMPLACENCY CANNOT BE TOLERATED"

(USAF Colonel Johnson, 7405 Support Squadron)

I seldom did much of anything I was told to do as a kid. Things in my house could be pretty tense but I really think I was one of those kids who was just contrary regardless. And I would fight anybody who tried to make me do anything, even if it was something I wanted.

So I didn't fit in well with my family. School was fun and I enjoyed learning. I was a model student, until puberty, that is. I realized as a freshman in high school that I was getting straight A's but zero friends. I figured I was really going nowhere. So by sophomore year I gave up on studies and had become the class clown. Popularity was paramount and school work suffered. I often rushed to just barely get homework done before class. I was well on my way to following the family tradition of alcoholism by the time I was sixteen years old: have a good time, become popular, and head toward a life of mediocre complacency (at best). But deep down I knew I was in trouble but had no idea how to get out of it.

I kind of left home at age sixteen. Would go for a couple months at a time, then back for a couple months, and so on. By eighteen I was about to start college on my own and didn't have a clue what I wanted to do or study. Ha! "Study?" Party and drink was more like it. By my second year of college I knew I could no longer keep it up so I dropped out. Got my draft notice within two days of giving notice to the university! But, being fearful of getting killed on the ground in Vietnam, I had already made plans to join the Air Force and hoped for some sort of desk job. Actually, I wanted to be a news reporter. The Air Force sent me to Basic Training and then on to Photo School. Case closed.

Two things happened to me around this time that forever changed me. First, I met "the" girl who later became my wife. Second, I had to stop drinking and become disciplined in the military. Finally, I had someone to live for and I had structure. I was twenty years old and lucky and grateful for both blessings.

I got married with no real prospects and no money. We had our first little girl shortly after while stationed in Great Falls, Montana. Could have been a million miles from what my wife and I were both used to but we had to make do. Had to! Before our daughter was a year old I was sent to Germany and I ended up flying on an air crew over East Germany and other places taking "spy" photos. Dangerous at times but a lot better than crawling on my belly in Vietnam.

Our flights were usually pretty routine, we would usually fly into Berlin, land, then fly out taking photos and "listening in." At the end of every pre-flight briefing our Squadron Commander made the comment that "Complacency cannot be tolerated." There were real risks. Every now and then we would encounter a Russian MIG fighter that would shoot across our aircraft's nose trying to force us out of legal air space. We would also be able to read the signature of a missile armed and locked onto us (often). During those tense political times many of us thought this might be the day they actually shoot us down. There were many days we were all scared and glad to be able to land safely. We had to stay alert.

But there are other scary things in life too.

I think every guy is really scared to death of babies. My wife, not allowing fatherly complacency, involved me from the day we brought our first daughter home. She made me care for our daughter, dress her, feed her, bathe her. I had to learn and fast!

Then my wife, always thinking of our future, pretty much made me go back to college and take some courses, any courses at all. Just get on with it and make something of yourself! "You can do it, Jack."

So the words of my Commander, "Complacency cannot be tolerated." really stuck.

Do something – anything. I mean it. Be alert to what's available. Try new things and you cannot be afraid to fail. You will fail sometimes but how will you ever know your boundaries unless you at least try?

I heard a very bright young exchange student from Italy speak this morning. She's returning home after a year in the U.S and she was relating her experiences. She made a comment also that fits in here really well. She said "How will you know what borders are unless you cross them?"

Do the tough things. And do your best all the time. It's hard at first but if you enjoy it and accept the challenge of it, you will find satisfaction, contentment, and happiness. Have you ever "zoned" out doing something and found that the time just flew by? Look for those things. Now it does take practice, I want to remind you of that. You cannot expect success right off the bat but you must try.

Try anything. Get up. Get active. Get involved. Get going. Go get it because it won't come to you. Complacency cannot be tolerated.

Pre Internet, pre television, pre-computers, pre-shopping malls, we actually had to work and think. We didn't have "apps." We actually talked with our neighbors and relied on them for help. We canned our own food. Hell, we even had gardens that we used to supplement our food sources. We picked weeds instead of spraying. We walked to school (and back!). We engaged with the real world face to face. And we got dirty. Doctors made house calls. In the winter we shoveled snow. In the summer we pushed mechanical lawn mowers and sweated. We rode bikes everywhere and played outside from sunup to sundown. Oh, and we didn't have seatbelts!

Sound like a different world? It was. And it wasn't all that long ago. If you're from certain parts of our country or you were born before 1955, you might remember some of this stuff or similar stuff. The United States was unmatched throughout the world. World War II and the Korean War were over. Nobody had the kind of strength or prosperity we had. "Made in Japan" meant junk. We had it all.

My parents bought a brand new house in Buffalo, New York in a very nice neighborhood for $13,000 in about 1952. A car cost about $1,000; maybe a little more for a really nice one. Gasoline was less than $.20 a gallon. Yeah, wages were comparably low too so I'm not saying things were cheap compared to now. I am saying that life was a lot simpler and a lot more "hands on." People handled things. People engaged with the world in which they lived. Manual labor meant something. And people were born and died in their neighborhoods. A vacation trip of a lifetime was anything more than 60 miles from home.

But we were all connected on a national level. We read newspapers and magazines. We listened to the radio. Imagine reading or listening to a news report that simply stated facts without sound bites or "commentary." We decided for ourselves and discussed things with our neighbors.

So what's different today? Almost everything! We have become slowly complacent. We rely on systems, on chemicals, on technology, on the government, on almost everything except ourselves.

What we have is great, I have to admit. I have three arterial stents in my chest and probably wouldn't be alive without them. No complaints on that front. But when I researched them and kept asking my doctor why this and why that he actually seemed off guard, not used to being questioned. In my bizarre way of thinking I actually believe that he works for me! After all, I'm paying him, aren't I? Oh, you say the insurance company is paying? Well, again, in my twisted way of thinking, I've hired them too as a business to cover my losses should I have need of medical services. I get pretty ticked off when a medical professional tells me I can't have something without the permission of my insurance company (i.e., my hired business partner). If you hired a painter and tried to buy paint but were told the store would first need your painter's permission you'd think they were joking! What's the real difference?

We don't seem to be responsible for ourselves any more than we are physically active. When we do go out somewhere now we even expect the doors to open automatically for us. Tried the stairs lately?

There is nothing wrong with modern advances and I'm not advocating living in the 19th Century although it does sound nice sometimes; until we remember smallpox plagues and shortened life spans. I'm all for new stuff but let's not forget that we may see them disappear one day. Let's at least learn a few basic skills, carry a pocket knife at least, and be aware of all these gifts that are in addition to our human nature. Try skipping some small convenience each day and appreciate that thing.

When you think about it, who gains the most when the population in general becomes complacent? Answer: those who seek power, money, or control over the population. If we don't question things it's like giving a "get out of jail free" card to those who would take away our world and shape it in their own image. Put some names and faces on this when you think about it: Many political office holders, large corporations, and religions. That last one, religion, will probably get this book banned and me in trouble but you have to ask yourself how many wars have been fought in the name of somebody's god? How many corporations create need for their products, needs you didn't have the day before? And how many politicians decide who gets what based on who pays them the most?

Yeah, there are good things (remember to stay positive) out there, really good things. But how many Saturdays do we spend cutting grass rather than learning some new skill that we don't even know might bring out our true calling in life?

You decide. That's the point. Complacency cannot be tolerated.

PART NINE
FUELING UP

We've talked about a lot of pretty simple processes and we've also talked a lot about attitude and outlooks on life. Talk is cheap but there is a cost to everything. If you are working on the things I've brought up in this book, doing the assignments, and doing a lot of thinking and soul searching, you are consuming energy. And unless you have some sort of energy source you will eventually run out of fuel, slow down, get distracted, fall over, and stop functioning in any purposeful way. I don't want you to fall over and stop.

I've found there are basically two kinds of energy required: long term and short term. If that's true then you need to have a long term source of energy and a short term source too. Kind of like solar energy that is slow and steady versus the head of a hammer slamming your finger instead of the nail. Oh yeah, a lot of energy gets released real fast when you do that!

The difference is the ability to go to work day after day, despite your mood, despite the current crises, and still find within yourself the ability to slog along and, overall, enjoy what you do and feel like you're making a contribution. That long term energy is in contrast with an immediate, personal, maybe painful or scary event that requires your immediate reactionary response, like when you slice your finger while cutting vegetables in the kitchen and you don't know where part of that finger is. (First-hand experience if you will pardon the pun!) It's amazing how fast you can move in a crisis compared to working out for an hour or two.

You burn fast or you burn slowly. Either way, you do burn up energy and you have to replace it and recharge.

There are other aspects to energy too: physical energy, mental energy, and spiritual energy. One feeds or reinforces the other and you need all three to be in balance personally.

The matrix I'm describing looks like this:

ENERGY	LONG TERM (PERSEVERANCE)	SHORT TERM (IMMEDIATE)
PHYSICAL	GENERAL STRENGTH AND ENDURANCE	BURSTS OF HIGH LEVEL WORK AS FOR A SHORT TERM PROJECT
MENTAL	PLANNING & DOING FOR THE FUTURE	SELECTING THE RIGHT RESPONSE FOR THE IMMEDIATE SITUATION
SPIRITUAL	OVERALL POSITIVE OUTLOOK AND CONFIDENCE FOR FUTURE SUCCESS	RESPONDING TO SITUATIONS DAILY THAT REFLECT YOUR LONG TERM POSITIVE OUTLOOK.

If you are out of balance you will not function at your true potential. Yeah, like almost everything else in this book, I learned this the hard way. So let me share what I've learned about this thing too. And there is no writing of lists required this time. But you do have to, once again, look closely at yourself and maybe a goal (well, maybe some list) will come out of it.

Here goes.

Physical Energy

Let's go into physical energy first. Get fit. Yep, it's that simple. Eat right and exercise. See your doctor regularly. Most of us do have crumby genes lurking in our bodies or, even if we have great genes, we tend to get older every day and physically deteriorate until…you know…it's over.

If it's so simple why don't we do it? I wonder how much is spent annually in this country on diets, exercise equipment, and healthcare. Estimates I've looked at put that number in the neighborhood of $3,000,000,000. Yeah, that's trillion! Maybe more. And the number is growing according to various fitness related company reports and the CDC. As that number grows so do our waste lines and our blood pressure. We are obsessed with it all but as a country in general we don't do it.

Now I have to admit that I can get hung up on "equipment" too. I enjoy bike riding. So I bought a pretty nice road bike, helmet, mirror, biker's shirts, padded gloves, toe cages, and, best of all, those padded (butt protecting) spandex pants! If you want to feel like an idiot get a pair of those and wear them around town. By the time I get all my stuff together, wriggle into the pants, pump up the tires, fill the water bottle, and get the helmet and mirror adjusted, it's almost time to be back home and the ride should be over!

No matter what your age, eat a proper diet but be sure to splurge once in a while; not to excess, but really "once in a while!" Too many people "yo-yo" diet by going from fad to fad depending on the most recent celebrity cook book. "Tryin' hard to be like Gary Cooper – Super Dooper!" Why on earth would some movie star influence you to eat according to their directions? Even those doctors who publish diet books are suspect in my mind as they also seem to come and go, cash their book royalties, or start TV shows (with ads for cheese dips and potato chips or some unhealthy fast food chain).

We seem to think that if we eat like the stars we will look like the stars and maybe be happy with ourselves. What we forget is most stars have personal trainers, work out in their private gyms up to six hours a day, at least four to five days a week, and starve themselves from time to time. That is, the skinny, good looking ones. Secret: It won't change your world!

Another secret: Some people are actually bigger or smaller than others. Wow! This "secret" might actually be worth whatever you paid for this book. We are all different. We are not even intended to be similar. No matter what you do you will be you, all alone with whatever family genes you inherited, wandering through life, with the body make up you were blessed with. Sorry but you have to face up to that. That's just the natural order of things.

But you do have a choice of what you put in your mouth; that is, as long as you think for yourself and don't respond to the almost constant barrage of fast food ads that surround us. You can't avoid the damn things.

Select foods that are healthy, as healthy as you're comfortable with. Don't suddenly change your eating habits because of some new promising diet. You won't last through it for the rest of your life. Change comes slowly, remember? If you weigh more than you think you should (in concert with your doctor or nutritionist – not some "chart" of what you ought to weigh) try one simple change. One. Get used to that one thing. Then maybe another when you're ready. Just stick to it. Think long term rather than 10 pounds a week. How about something like a pound a month? That's twelve pounds in a year! Not great but not bad either and certainly going in the right direction.

Maybe you don't weigh enough for whatever reason. Maybe you've been dieting and trying to look like a movie star and you do have the stamina to stick with it long term. Ok, but is it really the "right" weight for you and your life style?

Racial and cultural background plays a lot into our physical appearance, habits, and foods we tend to consume. If you're Chinese I don't really think you're never going to eat rice or fish again. If you're of German descent I doubt you will never have a bratwurst.

You are you, a product of your genetics and of your culture. So eat well to maintain your body in its own natural state.

It's all about "healthy" balance for you; not somebody else's targets. Make your healthy choices. Your diet is your physical fuel source so keep the machine stoked appropriately.

Given proper food intake, let's now turn back to physical conditioning.

Move!

It wasn't that long ago in human history that we actually walked most places and did manual labor just to eat, clothe ourselves, and stay reasonably warm. In other words, we moved, lifted, pushed, pulled, and shoved a lot of stuff most every day. Today? We move to another job, we operate lift machines, we truck, and we snow plow. Some of us just move a lot of paper or move our fingers around a touch screen or keyboard of some type. Maybe others of you flip burgers.

The result: Generally, we couldn't survive physically without our technology. In addition, we also have come to rely on our medical technology to keep us going when we get the shocking news from our doctors that we are diabetic or have chronic heart disease, or are just plain obese and putting so much stress on our joints. Take a pill. Have a procedure. We'll be fine.

I have never run a marathon nor do I live in the woods or hunt my own food or chop wood. I can't even tell you that I'm buffed up and physically fit. Not many of us can honestly say they are in good physical condition. But I believe, aside from my genetics and just my age creeping up, I'm pretty healthy and reasonably active. Could I be more so? Of course! So could you.

How? Oh, I'm so glad you asked!

First, take a realistic self-assessment of your physical condition. Once again, remember this is not about a particular weight or diet (everyone is different). This is about you and your self-assessment.

Can you comfortably walk up a flight of stairs? Can you walk a mile or two without gasping for breath? How's your balance? If it's not good it may be that your muscle tone is not what it should be. Can you do a few pushups? Now I don't know what age you are or what your physical limitations may be. I don't know your genetic makeup or what you may or may not be able to do physically. So you have to decide for yourself (kinda what this whole book is about).

Odds are, if you're reading this, you're not an Olympic or professional athlete, right? So, whatever you can do right now can be your starting point. To build both your mental and physical energy you have to invest in yourself physically. And an investment means you have to give up something now for a future return. If you invest in a stock you expect it will grow. You have to do the same for yourself. Invest some time and energy and I do guarantee that you will grow both mentally and physically. You will get a return on your investment.

If you're not used to routine exercise then just start small like a penny stock. If you already exercise routinely, then keep it up and consider adding to your routine if possible. But let's focus on those of you who aren't used to it.

Like the penny stock I mentioned, start small. One sit up or one pushup or one minute on an exercise bike or one flight of stairs or one anything will be a great start if you haven't done it before. Don't go join a gym or buy a bunch of workout clothes or equipment if you haven't routinely exercised before now. If you do you're missing the point and shifting the emphasis from "doing" to looking good and having "stuff." In other words, you're avoiding the doing part. (But you will have cool stuff for a garage sale later! Note how exercise stuff costs so much right after New Year resolutions are made and how little the "like new" stuff costs at garage sales the next summer.)

To get into a routine you can try the listing of things you can do when you are working on a goal and then just pick one thing to actually do. That goal has to be a SMART goal too. It has to be doable, measurable, and you have to make time to do it. Put it on your calendar or in your appointment book. It could be a minute or it could be an hour. It could be once a week or daily. It doesn't matter. Just start it and build a simple, easy habit.

By eating properly and routinely exercising you will be building both long term endurance as well as conditioning yourself for those times when you do need that burst of power. You will be storing both long term and short term energy.

Mental Energy

I find it absolutely fascinating that we are actually made of energy. Our bodies work on electrical and molecular level energy systems. Our brains function based on electrical and chemical networks in basically the same way as do our muscles. We are living, conscious machines made of the stuff of the universe itself. But, like all things, we won't remain in this state forever. We keep changing and churning our way through time and space. This state of being "alive" is only temporary but it can sure be a lot of fun or it can be painfully depressing. Being temporary creatures is a really tough pill to swallow when you think about it. But it is also the most wonderful gift imaginable. How you see it is really your choice, barring some bizarre situation.

Even war captives, deprived of basic physical freedoms and tortured unimaginably, have learned how to find fulfillment, even if only by using their own minds. Wasn't it Nelson Mandela who said while in his prison cell that his body can be captive but not his mind? "I am the master of my fate and the captain of my destiny."

There are many stories of creative prisoners who solved complex mathematical problems. I remember one in particular from the Vietnam War about an American captive, routinely beaten and isolated, who built his dream home in his mind. Finally, after the war and his eventual release, he actually built it and every measurement was precisely as he imagined it to be, down to the smallest detail.

That's power! Yes, an extreme example but you have that capability too – if you learn to develop it. Hope this book helps you do just that.

After you've begun to do that one physical thing take a deep breath and feel the sense of accomplishment. This is something you have achieved! It is a success and it is your start to better mental energy accumulation as well as physical. If you feel the exuberance and satisfaction, remember that feeling. Maybe consider even writing it down and putting it somewhere you can see it to keep you motivated.

I've found that the most difficult challenge in keeping up a new habit is after I've done it for a while. I start to lose that feeling of accomplishment, start to see it as a chore, and then tend to put it off for some reason. When that happens, however, I know I'm on the verge of breaking through and having it actually become a lasting habit. So when you don't feel like doing it please know that you are on the verge of this activity becoming a solid habit. You have to plow through the feeling of putting it off. And each time you overcome that feeling you will be building your mental energy potential even more because you are now not only moving and improving your physical self you are also building your mental ability to focus and actually get stuff done.

Don't worry, you will come out stronger and it won't take all that long either. After you get to the other side of perseverance you will wonder why you didn't do this before. It will no longer be difficult. It will be a natural part of the new, successful you and you will find you can build on this success. And there are many more to come.

Start small. Make it easy and doable. Just move a little more than you do now. Then add a little more. Over time you will build physical and mental strength for both short term and long term energy. You will build confidence and ability that will fuel you toward more and more positive energy driven results.

One step at a time.

Once you start to get that sense of accomplishment, no matter how small, you start to build self-confidence and that's also a mental power source. You start to tell yourself, "Hey, self, look what I can do. If I can do that I can also do this." In other words, your physical state starts to feed energy into your mental state in a positive way. This is the payback for the effort you put in up front. You grow. You get better. Your habits improve. You become more positive. You become a clearer thinker. Your success is well underway.

As you improve your energy sources by eating better, moving, and clearing your brain of the negatives, you are also in a great position to start investing in your brain capacity. This is where mental exercise comes into play. Read a book, learn a song, learn a magic trick, do a crossword, maybe take a class or, ah, write a book. Whatever. Learn more about things that interest you or about your company or about what your kids are interested in. Think and absorb as much as you can. You will find that once you open the door to inquisitiveness you will hunger for more.

And yet again, it doesn't have to be tough stuff or so challenging that you will drop it in a couple days. What's interesting to you?

By the way, it's easy to tell you what you should do. I hate using the word "should." You "should" do this or that. No way. Please understand that when I give advice and maybe imply or even use the word "should," my intent is that you "should" (there's that word…) do what you think you should do; not me or anyone else. "Should" is only a suggestion. The other phrase I hear (and probably use sometimes) is "you have to…." Actually, no, I don't and you don't either. Think for yourself. Decide for yourself. Evaluate my advice for yourself too.

Spiritual Energy

I am not a religious person but I've been told many times that I'm very spiritual. So many books talk about the need to develop the spiritual side of your personality and, it seems to me anyway, that they almost mean you're not a complete human without a spiritual aspect to your life. Then they equate spirituality to belonging to a church or some religion. Here's where I will once again probably piss off a lot of you and you may close this book and toss it. So let me clarify what I mean by spiritual energy and religion.

To me, with all due respect, religion is a man-made crutch used to justify, without any plausible logic, personal power and wealth (of the holy leaders) at the expense of others (the faithful followers). This is, to me, another ancient form of 1.) Explaining the "holy shit, what was that?" stuff that we just don't understand, like death or even just thunder. Some holy authority steps up with an explanation and we all say "amen." Then we can go to sleep knowing that our faith will save us from the thunder and we won't really die one day. And 2.) "Just do it." Don't ask stupid questions, just do as I say or there will be consequences like burning in hell for all eternity. In other words, when I say kneel, you kneel. When I say give me 10% of your earnings, you give 10%, and on and on. Just do it or face eternal consequences. Oh, and by the way, it's not me asking for this stuff, it's God himself. Yeah, right! Like you have a note from God telling you you're in charge today and how much the dues are.

Boy, won't I be surprised if I'm wrong? If I am I hope I get a few points at least for honesty.

I'm one of those "recovering Catholics" so that likely explains my attitude toward the Catholic Church in particular and religions in general. I was taught way too many contradictions. For instance, if you're not baptized you cannot go to heaven. Really? Kinda severe isn't it for all the good people in the world, including infants, who just happen to die without being baptized? That's a tough love God. Oh, wait, God is all loving. No, wait again. He won't let you in his house though if he knows you aren't in his organization. No, no, that's wrong too.

He loves and embraces everyone and all creatures. But he burns some of them too. It's all just too confusing – a lot like the policies and procedures of a complex government: manmade and self-serving.

Here's what I do believe (if you even care). What we call "god" is actually the entire universe and we are a conscious part of it all. It is infinity and we are a part of it. A spec in it. But we are a part and we have a place in it all. We can make choices if we wish to seek understanding. We can chose to see the wonder in which we exist and find the beauty and delve into the mysteries that surround us and live through us. We also have the choice to ignore it all and miss every opportunity to be in awe of what we are.

I'd rather lay in the grass at night and contemplate the stars than spend an hour in a church service. I'd rather watch a butterfly float on the wind than listen to a sermon. I'd rather see a wolf take down a magnificent elk to feed its pups than go to confession. I'd rather help a homeless person find a meal and comfortable bed than donate to a religious cause. I'd rather write this book to hopefully help someone be happy with themselves than meet the Pope. Honestly.

I do read the Bible. I do read the Tao. I do read other thoughtful, reflective literature and I do contemplate who we are and why we are. Those writings are the philosophy behind what others take as the mysteries behind religions. I take them as reflections of the natural beauty and power inherent in our minds.

So what will it be for you? I do agree we benefit from spiritual growth and that can certainly mean being active in your faith and your religion. But it can also mean simply developing your creativity in such things as art and music or maybe just long walks in the park watching ducks. I don't know but I do know there is a time and place for reflection of who and what and why we are here and why now. I believe every individual has some purpose in life, if only to be a chain to the next person or generation or maybe just to touch one other life in some small way. Something. You have some purpose too. You belong.

This is, to me, what it means to be human and aware of our special gift of ability to understand and even question what we don't understand. It is clearly the soft side of our existence and it also fuels our sense of well-being and boosts our energy just to know we are a part of this whole universe. If we see the world in a positive light we will tend to be more positive, more thoughtful, more insightful, clearer thinking, focused, and happier in general. Life is to be enjoyed or there wouldn't be so much beauty around us. Yeah, you could say just the opposite too but if you look around and see a lot of ugly crap, it usually comes from people who aren't thinking, don't have goals, and don't appreciate the gift of life they have been given. And that is really too bad. And people do pile up crap.

Long and Short Term Energy Working Together

So far, all this eating right, exercising, mental activity, and thinking about the stars mostly builds long term energy that keeps us fueled and running along smoothly at a comfortable pace. Mellow. How about short term energy?

Long term energy strategies tend to keep us going on a long term basis but there are times we need a real boost, a big old shot in the arm. Like when we are about to deliver a major presentation to a client or prospect, or speak up to that teacher or other authority figure that intimidates us. Or maybe asking that person you're attracted to out for coffee. Mellow, long term, isn't quite enough. You will want to kick it up a couple notches.

Sometimes your reaction in a crisis is automatically driven by your adrenaline. You don't even have to think; you simply react instinctively, like when someone, or you, gets seriously hurt. Time slows down if you even remember what you did. We're built to do that. Isn't that cool?

It's the other stuff I mentioned that is not a natural reaction for which you have to consciously pull up your reserve energy. Pump it up is another way of putting it.

So how do you prepare for and then call up that extra boost when needed to deal with those often stressful situations facing you in the now?

Preparing physically and mentally for the long term is your best source of reserves. You can tap into that strength, the self-confidence, and your spirit that you have built up over time. That's your storehouse from which to go get the instant energy you need. The key to getting it quickly is to pump yourself up quickly physically and mentally and with your spirit or conviction.

Football, although I really don't like sports analogies, happens to be a good example. (I'll give another non-sports one in a moment.) For the most part, it's a game of short bursts of energy, physical and mental and with conviction. Say, in contrast to chess (all mental) or basketball (sustained activity). So why do you think we have bands playing and cheerleaders encouraging the fans to make noise? Because it pumps up the players. Noise and encouragement. It all adds up to short term bursts of physical, mental, and spiritual strength.

You can do this for yourself. (Here's the non-sports analogy.) I've noticed that motivational speakers who physically engage their audiences do get your heart rate up and they certainly get your attention. They have you yell out something or stand up and jump or stretch or something, and you do feel better, upbeat, and more positive.

Think of the last time you were about to enter a stressful situation. Maybe had to give a presentation, confront someone, or make a call on a challenging new client. Wouldn't it have been great to have had that motivational exercise just before?

Recently, I had to call on a client as a knowledgeable consultant to assist his business. I do know a lot about management and supply chain and other stuff but I know almost nothing about his particular business. I was new to this and very nervous about making a good impression, let alone nervous about not looking like a total idiot. I needed a short term boost.

So on the drive to his office, in the solitude of my car, I yelled. Yeah, really! I kept yelling out as loud as I could things like "YES, I CAN DO THIS!" "TOP OF THE WORLD, MA!" and just things like 'WHOOP, WHOOP, WHOOP!" Now other drivers may have begun to call 911 but, honestly, I don't think anyone noticed as I was sure to keep my eyes on the road and windows up. By the time I got to my client's office I was on fire. I was really pumped up, excited about what I was doing there, and ready to go with all the confidence in the world.

I was my cheerleader, my band, my key to unlocking the positive energy I had stored up. (Oh, yeah, the meeting went great! Wouldn't have been much of a story if I had come out making a fool of myself. I would have put that into the section about failure being a positive experience.)

The point is that short term boosts of positive energy require something on your part to get your blood flowing. Jump up and down. Yell out positive sayings. Give yourself a pep talk.

Another method to combine with that is to paint a mental image of your success before you enter the situation. This also applies to your general goal setting. It helps make the outcome real in your mind before it ever happens and helps you focus. Not only that, you get to rehearse it and maybe several variations of it before it happens. In other words, you've done this a few times already (at least in your mind) so when you go "live" it won't really be your first time and, hopefully, you've anticipated a few things that you might run into that would otherwise have thrown you for a loop. You're ready! You're experienced! You're confident! And your mind has formed a pattern of success so when it meets the outside world it has already prepared you.

Many athletes (Oh, how I hate sports comparisons but I have to admit they do seem to apply!) visualize like this. They are practicing over and over in their minds and their minds pre-condition them to success. You can do this too.

Instead of dreading having to mow the lawn or do the ironing or whatever chore or task you dislike try to visualize it already done. The lawn looks freshly mowed and you can smell the fresh cut grass. The clothes are all hung neatly in the closet and they have that just washed, clean smell. You walk out of that difficult conversation with the sense of accomplishment and success you were going for. Imagine that!

This won't work 100% of the time but I have to tell you, it will work about 90% of the time if you do this mental imaging routinely. No, you won't always anticipate every possible outcome or monkey wrench that gets in your way but, given your sense of preparation and mental practice, you won't be totally blind-sided and your odds of achieving your goal will be increased significantly.

Once again, like just about everything, it takes practice.

One more energy booster for you: Laugh out loud! Smile at least! ☺

Did you happen to wake up in a bad mood or depressed about something? Day not going well? Try this.

Don't do this in front of everyone or they will think you've lost your mind. But go off somewhere private (I love the privacy I get when driving by myself.) and laugh out loud. Really, for no reason at all. Just start to laugh. Fake it if you have to, and in a little while you will find your mood will lighten up. If you can't get away by yourself, just smile. I know you won't want to but it won't kill you and it actually doesn't hurt. There is something about the physical action of laughter or just smiling that sends signals to your brain that tell it to lighten up and relax.

Somehow the physical act of smiling or laughing stimulates your brain to think everything is ok. Yeah, it may not be but the action and mental response helps you relax and once you've relaxed you tend to put things into perspective. Odds are, whatever is bothering you, it is not actually the end of your world. Relaxing also seems to buy you some time to reset your negative response into a positive one and that helps you begin to rationally deal with your problem.

Ha! Try it! Fake it if you have to but give it a try. A really good belly laugh does more good mentally and physically toward boosting your well-being and your positive energy. Did you know that Three Stooges movies are used in cancer therapy with positive healing correlations? That's got to count for something.

So those are all ways to boost and maintain your energy long term and short term. Basic stuff but you have to actually do it and practice it. Start by thinking about what you're eating. Move more. Prepare. Laugh and have fun.

Find a good joke and spread the laughter. Smiles, just as much as sour pusses, are contagious.

Oh, one more thing: Don't watch the news too much. It seems to be our repository of crappy information meant to scare us and make us worry (and buy whatever product the sponsor is pushing right after they make us worry and create a need for relief from that worry by buying their product. Really!)

PART TEN
NEEDING SOMEBODY SOMETIMES

There have been so many times I just wanted (actually, still do sometimes) to just be alone. Leave me alone, World. I think to myself that I could be a hermit up in the mountains in my cabin and come to town for provisions once every year or two. Worn bib coveralls, long hair, beard, smelly corn cob pipe, can you see it? But then I think I don't want to be away from my wife. Maybe she would join me. I like being with her. A dog too would be great. Yeah that would do it.

But I have children that I miss seeing. And their spouses. And I want to see those grandchildren. Every day would be fine with me even if only for a few minutes. Then there are a few friends I would want to see now and then to spend time with and talk.

I guess I could be a hermit if I moved my cabin closer to the town and had at least my family and a few friends around. Yeah, that could work. Oh, what if I needed a doctor or a whole hospital? What if the dog got hurt and needed a vet? I can still make this work if I move yet a little closer to town, maybe just a small city. Not too big.

As long as I'm near a small city or maybe on the edge of a big town, I could go out to dinner once in a while; get my car worked on. I wouldn't have to go to town once a year or so for my provisions, I could go to Costco or Walmart once a month. Then I could pick up other stuff too once a week.

Yeah, right. A hermit might sound good but for most of us it's a fantasy about just getting out of the busy environment and its challenges once in a while!

Maybe a nice escape from reality is valid now and then, but, come on, a hermit? Sounds nice, but really?

We are social beings and we do need others around us. I'm not good at making close friends, although I do treasure the few that I have.

Recall I grew up in a very dysfunctional family. I was going to say "raised" and tell you about my childhood but "raised" is too strong a word. I was pretty much ignored. I spent my childhood in a house more than in a family. We talked as little as possible, avoided everything of importance, and when something important was spoken about, it was in the form of yelling, usually slurred with alcohol and tainted with fear. It was always tense and I learned to avoid anything serious. Just get away if you can if anything starts up. Get out. Get away.

I don't recall ever being hugged just out of plain affection. Hell, I don't remember any affection or anyone saying "I love you." I do remember the yelling and I remember being told how smart I was or how strong I was or how I was going to go to college. But then I also remember getting beat up, being lousy at sports, hanging out with all the misfit unpopular kids (some with the black leather jackets). I remember other kids' mothers telling their kids to stay away from me. I remember motorcycles, leather jackets, carrying a knife, and trying to be tough. At the same time I went to the beach in shorts, tennis shoes, madras shirts, and listening to 60's surfing music. I didn't really "fit" anywhere, including home. I didn't know how to fit in and was, as I look back now, desperate for affection and guidance.

I dated a lot of girls when I was a teen and even had a couple serious girlfriends. But still, something was missing. They got possessive, too close, and I was too used to being alone.

I did go to college. I had no clue what I wanted to study and I had no help at all from my parents when filling out the application forms. My father actually refused to tell me his salary, a required entry for tuition assistance. "That's nobody's God damn business." So I made up a number and sent it in.

This was the early sixties and the height of the Vietnam War. And I was scared. I'd seen too many guys go to Viet Nam and come back really screwed up. I was also drunk now most of the time. I wasn't interested in school. And I had gotten to the point where I really just didn't care about anything. I was fed up with girlfriends and their petty manipulations, I knew I wasn't going to make it in school, and there really wasn't much point in going home any more. I did have a part time job in a hospital but I was older than most of the other kids there so I didn't fully fit in with that crowd either. And by now I'm going on twenty years old. A hermit's life was actually sounding pretty good.

I remember one autumn day driving out to the beach by myself just to think. What am I going to do? I sat alone on the beach for some hours. Cold. Windy. Lonely. Beaches on Lake Erie are great in the summer but in the fall they are desolate. Just as I was. How do I get out of this mess? Drink myself to death was a viable option. Honestly, I didn't really see any other. I sat there watching the water and feeling the cold wind and blowing sand for hours. Totally depressed and totally fed up with myself, I rode slowly back toward Buffalo.

I think that was the moment I subconsciously, completely unaware, started to seek something different. I didn't know what but I understood I couldn't continue the way I was. I quit trying to be something I wasn't. And I wasn't much but I accepted that for the first time.

Shortly after, things started to change. No, there was no planning on my part, no lists, nothing conscious. I think my realization of who and what I was became real for the first time in my life. I was heading nowhere, I wasn't happy with myself, and I didn't like it. It was time to leave all this behind somehow. I had no idea and no plan. But, for the first time, I was fully aware that I didn't like my life or who I was. I was fed up with it all.

Why am I telling you all this? Because I think this may have been the point at which I learned that the first step toward happiness and however you want to define success is when you first become "aware" that things aren't right with your life. You don't know why and you don't know where to turn but just by becoming aware something inside you changes. You are no longer just willing to go along with everything in your life. Something has to change. That's "aware." That's the starting point.

While this same sort of new attitude was just beginning to take shape, I met a girl just a few months after sitting and brooding on the beach. This one was different and had I met her before my change I probably would not have noticed her. In fact, we worked in the same group and everyone else knew her but I never did notice her. But when I did now, I was able to see how different she was. I couldn't have told you then what that difference was but I could tell she held all the things I was looking for. And she changed my life.

No, I didn't suddenly change overnight! That's why I can tell you from experience that change doesn't happen quickly. Awareness may start a process of change but you have to slog through it and it isn't easy. You don't suddenly give up all that you have learned, all you are from the time you're born, and run carefree through a field of daisies with the wind blowing through your hair while uplifting music is playing in the background. No. Change can be ugly. But you can change.

I dropped out of school, avoided the draft by enlisting in the Air Force and married that girl, all in about a year. She was just seventeen when we met; I was nineteen. She was the loving, caring, wise woman who gave me everything. Yeah, seventeen years old! I've never met anyone like her, ever. When we married she was eighteen and I just turned twenty one.

And then we had a baby!

Having help from somebody can make all the difference. After that, becoming responsible for someone or something else builds on that.

Think I wasn't scared to death? Talk about responsibility and getting the change of my life! But trust and love prevailed despite the odds against success. We have been married almost fifty years now, have three fantastic adult children and four grandchildren with whom we spend as much time as we can.

I think what I've learned (and continue to learn) spell happiness and success for me. Whatever your life is like or where you think you want to go with it, I know you can. I hope you have someone special in your life and I hope these stories, experiences, and techniques help you define your success and achieve it in spades.

All the techniques are great but perhaps the greatest single influence and source of encouragement as well as help came from other people. Some loving family, some very good friends, some just from helpful people who were willing to share and assist.

Look for those people and accept help and advice of those you trust. Do make your own decisions as not all advice is suitable to you or your needs or goals. But be accepting and consider all that comes your way. People do want to help others. Listen closely with an open mind. Somebody once told me to first seek to understand the other person's point of view, then, and only then, seek to be understood. Good advice. I think the well known author, Steven Covey, advocates this.

I really do believe that everybody has something to offer and good, even great, ideas that you can benefit from can come from the weirdest sources. You never know what will turn up from where or from whom. For that very reason you have to be alert as much as you can without prejudging people. I grew up not trusting anyone so this was a difficult lesson for me but as I look back over the years it may be the most valuable overall.

I got help from teachers, from counselors, from friends, certainly from my wife, from co-workers (bosses and employees), from people I thought were idiots (I was only generally right about them being idiots until I came to understand them), from books, classes, videos, even from my own children and my grandchildren. I recently watched how one of my grandsons performed a pretty simple task in a way that was far easier than the way I had been doing it. He was twelve years old at the time and teaching me a different way to do something very simple. Help is all around.

And that brings us to helping others and giving of yourself. If others are so helpful and caring, you can also find great joy in helping others and that opens the doors to even more experiences and insights and learning on your part.

So your next assignment is to discover something you believe in, and go give of yourself to it. No, don't write a check (although there is desperate need for money for many worthy causes). I really mean take on a project or take someone under your wing. You have unique skills that somebody else needs help with.

It doesn't have to be anything difficult; especially if you're not used to giving of yourself. Maybe it's just bringing used books to a local library. Maybe offering to assist in a classroom. Teachers always can use an extra hand. Maybe tutoring a child. Maybe it's just befriending that one person who always seems to be ignored. Maybe something simple to help in your church. I don't care what it is just as long as you do something small. And, like everything else in this book, build on it as your comfort grows. I don't expect you to become another Gandhi or Mother Teresa but at least look for opportunities to be helpful and just nice to other people.

I'm sure you can think of people who have helped you at least in some small way. Pay them back by spreading that idea of helping others. It's good for them and it is also good for you.

Have you ever considered writing those people who helped you a letter of thanks?

PART ELEVEN

SUSTAINING SUCCESS REQUIRES ACTION

Most self-help or motivational books seem to bring you to the achievement of a goal or success of some sort and then leave you there. Wow! You made it! It's been my experience that consultants tend to do the same thing. They come into your company or a personal consultant comes into your life, advises you on how to get what you want (or they tell you what you should want), guide you to it, then leave. And what happens? All is really good for a while and you're all hyped up and gung ho.

That lasts for a while until the next crisis or the next event in your life or the next book comes out. (Of course, you'll never need another after this one, right? Actually, I hope that's true.) You forget. You put all your 7 habits or 12 steps out of your mind and you drift off. Oh, yeah, you recall something. Yeah, what was that 3rd step again? Something about visualizing your goal or putting a sticky note on your mirror? Yeah, and what followed that? How many times have you or your business "solved" the problem at hand only to "solve" it again, and again, and again?

I think it's just plain dumb to not have a long range plan that can grow with you and is easy to do. Your life doesn't stop once you reach some goal or some measure of success. So why would you not have a flexible, living plan to guide you toward your next success? Why should your plan ever stop your ability to keep going forward? I believe successes build on each other. And, realistically, you and the world around you change all the time. If that's true then your best tools must also grow and change and be responsive to your needs today, tomorrow, and on into the future.

Think of a tree that grows from a seedling, spreads its roots, changes with the seasons, sprouts new branches, and is able to be flexible enough to bend with the wind but always follows the sun, accepts the rain and nutrients from the soil, houses birds, and maybe even provides not only shade in the summer, fruits in the fall, but can also even be a source of fun if you hang a swing on it. And it grows for generations. All this and it can be a source of real beauty as leaves change colors and the limbs grow into different shapes. Of course, there are some pretty ugly trees out there that are just a pain to maintain. I like ones that do all I describe and don't really need much maintenance. Simple is good.

So this next part is all about getting traction with your plans for success and, once underway, keeping it all together and supporting your growth. Ready? Here we go to wrap up all this stuff from the preceding pages, get you on track, and watch you grow and spread your branches.

Keeping Track / Keeping Score

Most businesses (Ugh! A business lesson? No, just an example of something that works. No accountants, consultants, or even computers required.) use what's called a "balanced score card." Its purpose is to identify just a few very key factors that describe usually four main areas of critical importance to the success of the business. Money is one (kinda have to have enough to function). Growth is another (learning new things and moving forward in your markets of interest), Customers (this is usually a measure of how you're doing in the eyes of those you serve), and Staff (usually how well your company is treating employees and nurturing and training them, those types of things). There can be other factors and even other uses of the Balanced Score Card.

It's actually pretty essential to assist in checking your critical performance periodically and I believe everyone should have some simple way of knowing whether they are on track or not. A good scorecard is simple and very easy to build and to interpret. If it gets too hard or too complicated it has missed the point of being like a weather monitor that instantly tells you what the weather conditions are. Your scorecard will also be simple, easy to construct, and be totally useful in a very meaningful way – for you!

So, how do you put one together for yourself? (This sounds like instructions are coming and it's not going to be as simple as he says it is.) Well, I have to admit, like everything, it does take some getting used to, some thought, and it does take some time now and then. But, once built, it will become second nature to you and guide your activities day by day, week by week, until you hardly give it a thought. It will become automatic and keep you on track as you happily go through your days.

First, let's talk about the hardest part: MONEY.

Your Money

I'll bet you don't have enough, right? Here's another secret: I do. You can too. The question really is, what is "enough?" We tend to think that Warren Buffett and Bill Gates and movie stars and CEOs have it all and only if we could make that kind of money we'd be happy. We play the lotteries. We enter sweepstakes. We even get pissed off when we don't get that raise we were counting on. I'm working with a large and growing company that needs to get its costs down and increase productivity to remain competitive and open for business. They've cut out overtime and many of their employees are really upset because they "counted" on that extra money when, in fact, it was never promised.

Also, consider that most domestic arguments and even the breakup of marriages and families are about money. Which is kind of dumb when you think about it. A divorce actually costs everybody more in the long run. I know I can't afford to be divorced; never could; never want to either.

Just as diet and exercise sound so simple but require some effort, so is a budget and living by it. So approaching an easy way to set up and stick to a budget is our number one item on our scorecard.

First, how much do you make? How much can you count on, in cash, each week or payday or month or whatever period you're comfortable with? I do suggest setting up your budget based on your cash income on at least a monthly basis. Once a week seems to be too often. I do mine twice a month in conjunction with when I get paid and receive income. So, once or twice a month usually works well.

Note that I said how much you can count on. That's a relative concept as no job or income is totally reliable. Who knows what could happen to your ability to earn and receive income in the future; even tomorrow? So what is reasonable keeping in mind your world of income may disappear? My wife was earning a pretty good income in a very responsible job one day and the next she became disabled. It does happen so you can never fully count on anything. That includes Social Security, retirement income, etc. So, as we work through this we'll also consider alternative incomes and insurance as we consider an uncertain future for us or for our loved ones who rely on us.

But for starters, keep it simple. If you get a routine paycheck count that. If you work on commission or you have an irregular income arrangement, figure out your high cycle, your low, then your overall annual average per period (monthly or twice a month). If you have irregular income allow for some reduction of that average in order to buy yourself some cushion. You might consider lowering that average by at least 10% for safety. If you have reduced too much you actually come out ahead in the long run. It's like savings for that cushion effect.

Ok, now you know how much you earn each period by dividing your annual cash income by 12 (once a month) or 24 (twice a month). Great! And maybe you've built in a cushion also. Wonderful!

Now, list all your liabilities, yeah, all of them. The obvious ones are rent, car payments, credit card payment, and other bills you get in the mail or on-line. The less obvious are the periodic ones like doctor bills or bills you might get for insurance that you pay once or twice a year. Then there are the even less obvious ones like Christmas or an anniversary or birthday. How about a vacation? How about auto or home maintenance? Then going on down the list, there is the cost of replacing that television or computer or that power tool or the fridge. Maybe replacing a furnace? And even more after that, what about routine expenditures like gasoline, groceries, going out to eat, getting a beer or a round of golf or going to the movies? The money all comes from your earnings, doesn't it?

If you're not sure what you are spending (and many people aren't – you're not alone here) then spend about a dollar for a pocket sized notebook, find a pen and keep both with you all the time. Each time you buy or spend anything write down the date, what it was, and how much. You can round it to the nearest dollar if that's easier and faster for you. The results can be eye opening! Many people learn that they had no idea they were spending so much on things they really didn't need or even want. When you see how much you're spending and what you're spending it on it can be shocking.

The point is you must know how much you earn and how much you spend on everything throughout the year and allow for it each pay period. Then by setting an appropriate amount aside each pay period to allow for all expenses, even those that only come along once or twice a year, you can see what things actually cost pay period by pay period. In addition, it takes the pain out of that one big payment if you've been putting money aside bit by bit to fund that one big payment or have built a buffer for those unexpected expenses.

By tracking what you actually spend you also take the guess work out of building a realistic budget. Most people will way underestimate what they actually spend on stuff. You won't if you keep track. And you don't need to do this usually for more than a month or two at the most. You will probably be shocked by how much you actually spend on unnecessary stuff that add no pleasure or value to your life. But you have to be honest and thorough about it or you're only kidding yourself. (Remember, this isn't all that hard but perseverance can be.) If you have a spouse and children, try to get them to do this at the same time and share it all.

Following is an example from my own budget (I made up the numbers to make it simple but you can use this as a template.

The basic format is:

YOUR NET INCOME PER PERIOD (Cash - Not What Your Paycheck May Say As Earned)

MINUS YOUR FIXED EXPENSES (Per Pay Period)

MINUS YOUR VARIABLE EXPENSES (Variable Expenses Can Include Your Discretionary Expenses)

MINUS YOUR SAVINGS OR SET ASIDES FOR FUTURE EXPENSES

MINUS AN ALLOWANCE FOR A SAFETY NET (The 'What If'' Stuff)

EQUALS YOUR RESULTING INCOME LESS ALL YOUR EXPENSES (And This Number Should Be Positive)

An example follows on the next page with made up numbers to keep it simple (Don't worry, we'll walk through this is some detail):

1ST of Month	15TH of Month	SOURCE	ANNUAL	
$1,500.00	$1,500.00	Paycheck	$36,000.00	
$75.00	$0.00	Annuity	$900.00	
$1,575.00	**$1,500.00**	**TOTAL**	**$36,900.00**	
SAVINGS & SET ASIDES				**DUE**
$40.00	$35.00	Taxes	$900.00	15-Apr
$85.00	$75.00	Insurance	$1,920.00	3-30 / 9-1
$5.00	$5.00	Car tabs	$120.00	15-Aug
$25.00	$35.00	Car Maint	$720.00	?
$15.00	$15.00	Car Ins	$360.00	30-Aug
$0.00	$8.00	Club Fee	$96.00	15-Oct
$65.00	$75.00	MD Bills	$1,680.00	?
$0.00	$10.00	Birthdays	$120.00	several
$25.00	$25.00	Christmas	$600.00	20-Dec
$60.00	$60.00	Fun Out	$1,440.00	?
$100.00	$100.00	Buffer	$2,400.00	?
$420.00	**$443.00**	**TOTAL**	**$10,356.00**	
FIXED EXPENSES:				
$500.00	$500.00	Rent	$12,000.00	1st
$130.00	$0.00	Cable	$1,560.00	10th
$0.00	$125.00	Phone	$1,500.00	25th
$630.00	**$625.00**	**TOTAL**	**$15,060.00**	
VARIABLE EXPENSES:				
$75.00	$100.00	Credit Cards	$2,100.00	1st / 5th
$75.00	$70.00	Gasoline	$1,740.00	?
$150.00	$150.00	Misc	$3,600.00	?
$80.00	$80.00	Lunches	$1,920.00	?
$125.00	$0.00	Utilities	$1,500.00	25th
$430.00	**$300.00**	**TOTAL**	**$10,860.00**	
TOTAL ALL SAVINGS & EXPENSES:				
$1,480.00	**$1,368.00**		**$36,276.00**	
TOTAL INCOME LESS TOTAL EXPENSES:				
$95.00	**$132.00**		**$624.00**	

Now, let's take a closer look. Obviously, if you've entered all your reliable income and you've entered all your expenses, wherever you may have put them (more about that in a moment), look at the difference on the bottom line, "TOTAL INCOME LESS TOTAL EXPENSES." These should be positive numbers. If they aren't you need to act right away as you are spending more than you make. And that's not a good scenario. But we can fix that too.

After income, I start with putting money into savings. Most people don't but I find this works well for me. I actually put this money aside in a savings account associated with my checking account. This allows me to easily move money between savings and checking as needed. By putting money aside in savings it also helps keep me from overspending if the money is available in checking.

For your budgeting purposes, it doesn't really matter in the long run as long as you are keeping track. Most people will start with "FIXED" expenses and it's important to know the difference between "FIXED" and "VARIABLE" expenses as you set up your budget. So let's start with that.

FIXED EXPENSES

A "FIXED" expense is one that is the same all the time and typically due routinely over a long period of time, like once a month, for five years. Examples would be car payments, house payments, life insurance premiums, a fixed loan, a bill you cannot change and won't go away in the short term. In other words, these are expenses you're stuck with, "Fixed." Be aware you can do something about them, but usually only with great effort and in the long term. You could sell your car and buy a less expensive one. You could find a place with lower rent. You could refinance or even sell your house and move to something less expensive. None are easily or quickly accomplished.

VARIABLE EXPENSES

Unlike “FIXED” expenses, “VARIABLE” expenses change all the time but are routine and usually payable monthly or in some similar time period. Utilities are a good example. You may get a monthly water bill but it changes depending on the amount of water you used in the prior period. Phone bills are similar.

Notice that I put credit card bills into “VARIABLE” expenses. I did that because I’m assuming you get credit card bills and you pay off only what you can afford that month. And, of course, as you use a credit card, the balance due changes and so does the payment requirement. The ultimate goal would be to eliminate this expense all together and we’ll talk a bit about that too later on.

When you budget a variable expense you can only guess at the amount and, over time, take the average amount due. I strongly suggest using a number a bit higher than the average amount or even using the highest amount you’ve had to pay during the past 12 months. You will probably pay something less than this but if you allow for the maximum you won’t have any surprises and you will be building a bit of reserve against the “what if” stuff.

Variable expenses are something you do have some control over and can help you change your bottom line number in a positive direction. For instance, you can turn the heat or air conditioning down a little. You can use a bit less water. Certainly, you can reduce your credit card spending. In the example, I also used gasoline and lunches. These are things to consider when you are budgeting and actually spending and can pretty easily be reduced. Instead of buying lunches, how about bringing one to work? Getting your car tuned up can save on gasoline or, even if purchasing a car or truck, looking for fuel efficiency can cut that bill significantly. Do you take unnecessary and extra trips to the store or elsewhere in your car? Planning your driving errands can save you a bundle in the course of a year and you can lower your variable expense budget here.

So, "VARIABLE" expenses can be things you have some or even a lot of control over. You might find you can even eliminate some. But they do change every month. Note also that I've put on the budget when they are usually due. This all helps me plan out each pay period in case I haven't gotten the bill yet so I know it's coming before I get paid again. I've also used a "?" to indicate those items that are ongoing and don't have any particular due date.

SAVINGS

"SAVINGS" is the next big item to address. This is where you have a lot of discretion about when, which pay period, you put aside the money you will need in the future. In other words, if the first pay period bottom line is negative but the second is positive, you can move any savings line amount from the first to the second pay period and make both positive.

I calculate those once or twice or even bi-monthly bills down to a per pay period or per month amount and put that amount away into a savings account per my budget. That means, if I have a bill due once a year and I decide to put away a portion of that expense once a month, I simply divide the total I expect to need by 12. When the bill finally arrives, I have all the money I need as I have been putting some away each month anticipating getting that bill and I'm not caught short that month or end up borrowing money to pay the bill.

These accounts in "SAVINGS" can be fixed or variable. If variable, I allow the maximum I expect that bill will be and put that much aside. When the bill does come I'm usually pleasantly surprised that I actually have a bit more put aside than needed. When that happens I can move the excess into some other line item or use it to pay off some other bill that I might be trying to eliminate. Sometimes, we just go out and celebrate!

Notice also, that in the "SAVINGS" accounts there are things that are not bills. They are allowances for going out, birthdays, holidays, saving up for car maintenance, and other similar things. These are expenses I know I will have or things I want to save up for. What happens is that I become aware of how much I've put aside, say, to go out to movies. I can then decide when the mood strikes my wife and me to go out to dinner and a movie whether I can really afford it or not. This helps me keep from over spending.

I also have an emergency fund that I have in my "SAVINGS" accounts. Last year our roof sprung a leak and I had to replace the entire roof. Fortunately, I had almost enough cash in savings to pay for it all and with just a bit of belt tightening for one month, I was able to pay cash for the roof and borrow no money! Stuff happens so it makes sense to be as prepared as possible.

Moving From Negative to Positive

So that's a simple budget. It works great on a spreadsheet but you can do this on a sheet of paper too with a calculator or just add and subtract numbers. Remember, rounding to the nearest dollar or even five dollars is not as accurate but can work also and makes it really simple.

All this assumes that your Bottom line numbers are positive. When they are you can juggle when to put money aside, how much, for what, etc. You have freedom over your financial life.

But what happens if your numbers are not positive? I hate to use the word “Negative” but that is what you have – a lot of negatives to deal with.

Ok, so you at least know what your situation is to start. Freedom in this world, at least to me, is being debt free – not owing anyone for anything more than you can afford. It helps you sleep at night and eliminates a lot of worry, stress, ulcers, short tempers, and even boosts your self-esteem and confidence.

Once you’ve gotten your numbers down on paper there are a lot of things you can do to change negative numbers into positives. But you will have to work at it.

First, look at those “VARIABLE” expense items. Anything you can reduce here immediately increases your bottom line toward positives. Simply put, the more you reduce your expenses the more money you will have. I have to mention that increasing your income will do the same but changing jobs can be risky, raises and promotions are uncertain, and, frankly, if you’re currently in the negative that’s probably a reflection of poor spending and saving habits. If that’s the case, an increase in income must mean that you will not increase spending at all.

Admittedly, a negative bottom line could be very legitimate like some catastrophic expense that nailed you to a wall. If that’s the case, just keep plugging away. You will make it out to the other side in time.

Either way, expenses are the focus and reducing or even eliminating them are the keys. Start playing with those numbers first and see how you do. If you get to positive bottom lines, great. If not, keep looking. Go next to those “SAVINGS” items. What can you reduce or eliminate there? Remember some of these are simply money you put aside for personal items like Christmas or birthdays or saving up for something. If you reduce these your holidays might be a little or a lot simpler or you will have to put off buying that new item. After you've considered those reductions, how does your bottom line look?

If you have to keep going deeper into reductions, you'll have to take a look at what your other expenses are in "SAVINGS." Can you go a little deeper? If you reasonably cannot, you're going to have to go look at those "FIXED" expenses. Maybe moving to a less expensive apartment or shopping for some alternative source of phone service is a good idea. In fact, do you really need the service you're paying for? I know one very astute family who realized that they were paying monthly for cable service but hardly ever using it. Are you getting the value you are paying for? If not, get rid of it or at least reduce it.

Credit – The Black Hole

Let's talk about credit cards. They are the blood suckers of our financial social society. BLOOD SUCKERS! And they can suck you dry in no time at all.

When I was young I only used cash. Because of my knack to save I always seemed to have more than enough cash and I had a savings account. But I had no credit. Early in our marriage my wife suggested we establish credit. I was appalled! Why would we ever need to borrow money? Her response: "Do you ever want to buy a house?" She was right. Without credit history you can probably not come up with enough cash to buy those really large purchases in life, like a car, a house, maybe some major repairs, or even a particular medical bill. There is a place for credit; just like the universe seems to have a legitimate need for black holes. Notice though that our earth and most stars don't fall into black holes routinely. (Good thing for life on earth!)

If you don't already have a credit history I suggest you start one, but only if your bottom line on your budget is positive numbers. If you're already behind the eight ball you don't want that fact reported to the credit bureaus, right? Get your numbers into the black and then think about credit.

Start small. I do mean small; like a credit line of less than $1,000 or even a store account. Buy something inexpensive ($100 or $200) and then make payments over a period of 6 months or a year. Yeah, your interest will be pretty high and that small purchase will end up costing you more in the long run but you will be establishing the fact that you can pay reliably over a period of time. You will have a credit history. Do not miss a single payment though! If you do, that will show up as a "slow pay" or "late pay" on your credit report. There is a huge credit reporting network out there and they don't miss a thing.

Be aware that you should not have more credit available to you (even though you don't use it) than you can afford. The credit bureaus assume you will borrow the maximum amount available to you and they judge how you will be able to repay it reliably. The companies that extend credit will give it to you so easily that it's easy to get too much too fast. Please don't get sucked in.

Once you've established credit you can get your credit score for free by going on line and you really ought to take a look once in a while to know where you stand and to be sure someone else hasn't stolen your good credit.

My wife and I each have credit in our own names. Here's why: If all our credit is in both our names jointly, and something should happen to either of us, the other may be shut down and not have access to the credit account. It also creates a sense of independence financially and makes each of responsible for our own money management.

My wife and I handle the tracking of our credit purchases differently. When she uses her card she actually writes the amount charged into her check register. In this way, the money is “spent” before she even gets the credit card bill. Actually, it’s put aside and when the bill arrives she has already put the money aside. She pays the entire amount due and never pays interest on the credit bill.

I take all my credit card receipts and once a week I record them, add the total amount spent, and put that money into my savings account. Remember, I keep a number of expense account balances in my savings so I don’t actually have to go to the bank or even my on line banking. I put the amount due for the credit card into the savings account set aside to pay the credit card bill and subtract from the other savings accounts until I have the total required to fund the credit card account. When my bill comes, I move the credit card money from savings to checking and pay the entire bill; also never paying interest.

Now, my wife and I have long established credit so note that we pay the entire balances each month. We also selected a credit card company that gives us maximum air miles so we get to take trips at highly discounted fares. The point is, we don’t carry much cash any more, we earn miles, we don’t pay interest or late fees, we watch what we do spend closely, and we each have credit ratings in the high 800’s. We carry a $0 balance and only have two cards each that we ever use: Costco and a Visa for her, Lowes and a Visa for me.

Sounds good but you're not there yet? I have to tell you we were getting sucked into the black hole also at one time but there is a way out. Yeah, I was actually borrowing from one card to pay another despite all the advice we always hear otherwise. I had lost a pretty good paying job and we had to sell our beautiful house in a great neighborhood in one city where housing costs were low and move to a new job that paid about half what I was earning previously. And for the same amount of money for the house we were selling, we basically got not much more than a shack that was moldy, flea infested, dirty, and stunk. At around the same time our two daughters were getting married and our son was going off to college. Tons of lost income, major reduction of housing value, and high expenses. But the bills we had previously were mostly the same. I could not support all of it on my new meager income. The income example I showed above is actually higher than I was earning! And I had run up a bunch of credit card bills!

So we had to get things rearranged and under control. The first thing to do in such a situation or anytime you want to get out from under debt is to identify a single debt target you're going to go after with a vengeance. I mean pretend you are Attila the Hun and you're going to burn and pillage this debt town! You're going to wipe it off the face of the map!

To do this you will want to focus on the one you can pay off the quickest and get the most leverage from. What do I mean by leverage? Which one will give you the most cash when paid off so you can use (leverage) that cash to pay off the next. Now while attacking that one, you have to stop using the others or you're only shifting the battle.

For example, you have three debts you want to pay off:

Company A you owe $2,500 and your payment is $135/month and the interest is 12%.

Company B you owe $1,700 and your payment is $50/month and the interest is 15%.

Company C you owe $4,700 and your payment is $45/month and the interest is 17%.

Let's look closer. Remember, you have to stop using other cards. (Can't say that often enough!)

If you pay off Company A you get $135 extra per month when it's paid off, Company B, $50, and so on. You might be tempted to say pay off the 17% first but hold on. Let's look at the time and leverage.

Company A payment is 5.4% of the amount owed and it is 59% of all your payments.

Company B payment is 2.9% of the amount owed and is 22% of all your payments.

Company C payment is 1% of the amount owed and is 2% of all your payments.

Without even considering interest, which would be best to pay off? Company A is the way I would do it. The sooner I can get that $135 per month I could add that to my next targeted debt (company B) and get that one off the books really fast by paying them the current $50/month plus an extra $135 that I'm now saving from no longer paying company A. So I would pay only the minimums on B and C and put any extra I possibly could on the payment for company A.

I do look at the percentage of the payment compared to the amount owed; not at the amount of the payment. That way, I'm getting the most leverage, or the most cash in relation to the debt when paid off. The only time I pay much attention to the interest is if the payments are pretty close. I'll then work on paying off the one with the higher interest rate.

Of course, this assumes you stop using credit from Company A (and the others too until you get back under control – did I mention that?).

There are tons of books written about finances and this is not one of them. I'm trying to keep this to simple basic topics that will help you succeed in general. So enough about your money, debt, and credit for this book.

I believe that to be free of debt and getting to a bottom line that is positive, as well as creating buffers and savings, will help you get to a point at which you really feel you have enough money to live the life you wish to live. Again, this is all about the world according to you and your standards; not Bill Gates or some movie star. Managing your money is a key to a successful lifestyle.

One final thought here: Keep your check book balanced. If you're not sure how, most bank statements have a worksheet on the back of their statements. If you're still not sure, ask your bank.

Tracking Your Successes

Finally, we're getting back to your goals and your action steps. Remember about goals being "SMART?" This is the measurement and timed part of that. Go back now and take a look at one of your goals and your completed action plan. There should be some sort of measure, even if it's just "Yes, done," or "No, not done." And there should be at least a "Done By Date." You may have much more like percent increase or time saved or an amount of money or something but I'll assume you at least have some basic measurement and some basic sense of time to complete a step or steps.

This part is only keeping track of those numbers and charting your progress. A "report." Simple enough? It is but most people skip this part in the day to day activity of life. If you're going to really focus and stay pumped up on achieving your goal or goals, this is probably the best way to do it in the long run. Set yourself a routine "reporting" period to collect and write your progress.

A few things will happen if you do this.

First, it will keep your goal and action steps on your mind. This helps you keep it real and in the "now." It helps your subconscious continue to work on solutions that you may not have thought of consciously before. It keeps it all fresh and current.

Next, if you set aside a time and a place to "report" your progress to yourself, you're engaged in the reality of your progress. Your action steps are not just ideas or "wouldn't it be great if…." They are real and actionable.

Also, this helps you stay on track when things don't work out as you planned. Yeah. It helps you learn what does work and what doesn't. There are always unanticipated obstacles that pop up that require you to change course and try new things and take new directions toward achieving your goal. This helps you recognize course corrections when things do challenge you. You will be able to recognize them and take new actions or modify actions pretty much right away.

And, this report will show you what works and what isn't working. Just to be able to identify that helps you question why things are working and why things aren't. You will want to build on those things that are moving you forward toward your goal and you will want to consider why other things are not and what to do about those things. Maybe you need to change how you go about those things that aren't working or maybe get some sort of reinforcement against them somehow. Or maybe just drop them if they really aren't working and you can't make them work. Maybe they were too aggressive or you don't have the skill or resources you need to accomplish those steps. This knowledge now allows you to consider what to do about them.

Finally, being able to watch your progress, step by step, is just flat out encouraging. You can see a series of successes rather than waiting for who knows how long to reach the finish line. Without acknowledging those small successes along the way you get tired or even bored and tend to give up altogether before you even get close to the finish line. Seeing your progress on paper tends to make it seem real and tangible. It also gives you a chance to go back to prior reports and you may even be able to put some numbers on a graph to really give you a visual look at how you're doing. It gives you a sense of control too as you move forward.

Try different ways of tracking and reporting. You'll find it encouraging.

Slow It All Down

Good progress or poor progress is still progress. Knowing where you are helps you fine tune your progress and keeps you sailing along.

Imagine a goal like losing 20 pounds. Pretty common goal in this country. One of mine too. Which is easier: Losing 20 pounds in six months and keeping it off thereafter? Or, losing 1 pound every two weeks and allowing 12 months to lose the weight and then keeping it off thereafter? Racing to achieve any goal may be exciting and sound good but does it give you the time to alter your habits and to reinforce your successes along the way routinely? Reaching an aggressive goal too fast may be a great rush but this part of the book is about sustaining change.

How many times have you seen someone achieve some sort of goal only to then move on to another and forget all about the first? I've seen it (and done it) way too many times. Get the yard looking great. Wow! It looks great! Ok, what's next? Forget about the yard? No, we want to keep that yard looking great (if you want to in the first place) and accomplish another goal without letting the yard turn brown and grow weeds. We want to build on our successes. And to really do that slow it all down so you have time to build those new habits that will keep you going after you reach your goal.

Success doesn't happen quickly.

Your Score Card

We're coming to the end now and that's where you put it all together. I think the most important thing to consider is how aware you are of who you are and how you want to satisfy yourself and those with whom you wish to share your life. Well, ok, that's three things.

However you want to become aware and stay in that state is up to you. I've offered insights and shared some of what I've learned over almost 7 decades of a life which started out looking pretty bad to becoming a loved, happy, and, in my mind, wildly successful individual. I'm completely satisfied with my life and I look forward to more and more of it. I wish the same for you; mostly, happiness.

Life has its challenges to be sure but most are able to be overcome and you can even find ways to benefit from them.

To help you become and stay aware and, of course, to sustain your successes, your score card will probably address the following areas:

- YOUR LEVEL OF AWARENESS OF WHO YOU ARE
- YOUR RELATIONSHIPS WITH OTHERS
- YOUR FINANCES
- YOUR GROWTH AND ACHIEVEMENTS

One last suggestion here: You can set goals around each of these aspects. You can track them by writing them down. You can put scores on them and even graph them if so inclined.

Keeping a Journal of your thoughts is another option and helps support your growth and helps you identify how you think about each of those aspects of your life. If nothing else, keeping a journal is a very personal and private way to put your feelings and observations on paper. Written words are useful in getting things out of your head where they may be just fuzzy impressions and attaches specific meaning to those fuzzy impressions. They make you think and deal with who you really are.

PART TWELVE
ENJOYING YOUR SWEET SUCCESS!

In wrapping up this book I hope you realize that much of the perspective centers squarely on you and your happiness. Yes, it does talk about connecting with others but it does so in something of a selfish manner. What are you getting out of the relationship or the help others provide? Yes, it also suggests you reach out and help others but, while important throughout your life, that's a very minor theme within these pages.

I do believe that if you don't take care of yourself, know yourself, and feed your own happiness, you will never truly be happy or content or realize that sense of success I'm talking about. There are times to surrender to the desires of others either because you have to in order to keep a job for instance or to satisfy the needs of a loved one. But those still are personal choices. They are like gifts that you give of yourself. They may not be what you want nor even make you slightly happy but you give them thoughtfully for the good of another and, in that, you become happy by sharing of yourself.

This is in contrast with giving so much that you can't stand it and you lose your own identity. You get lost in the wishes and desires of others to the point you don't exist as your own person any more. I've seen it happen and it will drive you crazy if you allow this to happen. It can become toxic and you will never find happiness in a relationship like that. Move on. Find yourself.

Being aware, establishing priorities, setting realistic goals, and doing your action steps all contribute to achieving success on your terms. Aligning your attitudes, beliefs, relationships, and habits round it all out. I believe it is possible to achieve almost anything you are capable of if you plan it, visualize it, follow your plan, and learn from your mistakes as you grow and progress.

If you can get into a frame of mind before you even start, a positive attitude, you will already be on your way to your success. Whatever you believe of yourself will be your future. If you believe deep down that you cannot, you will not. If you believe you can, you will. Start by smiling and repeatedly, daily, maybe even hourly, telling yourself you can, then you will arrive sooner.

OK? Take a deep breath. Smile. Positive thoughts. Ready? Go get 'em!

I sincerely hope this book helps you in some way. No, I don't do everything I recommend every day and you shouldn't worry if you don't either. But I do them often enough that I tend to learn something new almost every day and my life just gets better and better. I am sincerely grateful for this gift of life; especially since I was pretty much doomed to mere existence early on. So I have to give thanks.

ACKNOWLEDGEMENTS

This is the part most readers skip as it is really kind of self-indulgent when a writer acknowledges and thanks people you probably don't know. But no book can exist without help from others. So here goes.

First and foremost, Jean, my spouse and partner for going on fifty years, I love you and thank you for being the source of my happiness and success. Without you I wouldn't be here at all. You taught me what family really means.

With Jean's wisdom, love, and guidance, my children taught me responsibility first, then laughter and the meaning of family. I continue to learn from them often and admire each of them for being themselves and overcoming their challenges in life. Thanks for putting up with my inexperience and trusting me (at least some of the time) and questioning me other times. Now, I'm discovering new ways of seeing things yet again through the eyes of my grandchildren. Like I've said, life just gets better and better.

There are a few special helping, caring friends I met along the way who gave me help when I needed it or were just a smile of encouragement. They include Sister Michelle of St Martin's grammar school in Buffalo, New York. She was kind to a screwed up young boy. Jim Napiers, my high school buddy.

We'd talk for hours about everything teenagers talk about. Sr. Rita Orleans, who gave me a chance to succeed by being myself and saying what was on my mind. Terry Radcliffe who encouraged me to continue my education. Spencer Smith who also let me be myself and helped me learn I was pretty good at what I did. Tim Sayan, who took a chance and hired me when I really needed to find a new job. Patty Cochrell, who welcomed me to a new world and gave me a hug when I really needed one. John Reich who kept encouraging me to write my book. To Austin Ross, my hiking partner who, once again, allowed me to talk like a grown up teenager.

There are so many more people, some unknown to me, who taught me so much all along the way. Thank you all.

Finally, to all the people who injured me along the way and robbed me of my happiness, I'm ok with it all. I now understand you and I thank you also for being in my life to help me push toward a better life. My father was really a good man in a bad circumstance. So was my mother. Not their fault for who they were or the times in which they lived. Rest in peace. May my brother also rest in peace. "Tomorrow is day one." And to my sister, you might be one of the very few who actually read this so let me also acknowledge you. I understand you better knowing more about how mom and dad neglected you too.

My best to you all.

Jack

BOOK JACK GALLAGHER FOR SPEAKING ENGAGEMENTS OR PERSONAL COACHING

Jack Gallagher has spoken to both large and small audiences and guided many individuals to a fulfilling, productive, and satisfying life. He will share his experiences and tips on personal success and leadership with your audience too.

For more information you can contact Jack Gallagher at soundachieve@wavecable.com, or visit either www.soundachieve.com or www.readitsyourchoice.com.

REFERENCES (AND SOME GOOD READING IF YOU'RE INTERESTED)

"Attitude Is Everything," Harrell, Keith D., 1995, Kendall/Hunt Publishing Co., Debuque, Iowa.

"Civilization, the West and the Rest," Ferguson, Naill, 2011, Penguin Books, New York, New York.

"Don't Sweat the Small Stuff…and it's all small stuff," Carlson, Richard, 1997, Hyperion, New York, NY.

"First, Break All the Rules," Buckingham, Marcus & Coffman, Curt, 1999, Simon & Schuster, New York, NY.

"Follow This Path," Coffman, Curt & Gonzalez-Molina, Gabriel, 2002, The Gallup Organization, Warner Books, Inc., New York, NY.

"Goebbels' Principles of Propaganda," Doob, Leonard W., undated, Public Opinion and Propaganda.

"Good to Great," Collins, Jim, 2001, HarperCollins Publishers, Inc., New York, NY.

"Life's a Marathon," Jones, Matt, 2007, Dreams Unlimited Publishing, United States.

"Smile! It Could Make You Happier," Wenner, Melinda, Scientific American, Oct 14, 2009, Scientific American, a division of Nature America, Inc.

"Subliminal: How Your Unconscious Mind Rules Your Behavior," Leonard Mlodinow, 2012, Pantheon Books, New York.

"The 5 Best Decisions the Beatles Ever Made," Stainton, Bill, 2008, Little Creek Press, Seattle, Wa.

"The 7 Habits of Highly Effective People," Covey, Stephen R., 2004, Free Press, Division of Simon & Schuster, Inc., New York, NY.

"The Happiness Advantage: The Seven Principles of Positive Psychology That Fuel Success and Performance at Work," Achor, Shawn, 2010, Crown Publishing Group, Random House, New York.

"The People's Common Sense Medical Advisor in Plain English; or, Medicine Simplified," Pierce, R.V., 8th ed., 1909, World's Dispensary Printing Office, Buffalo, NY.

"The Power of Habit: Why We Do What We Do in Life and Business," Duhigg, Charles, 2012, Random House, New York.

"Twilight of the Elites: America After Meritocracy," Christopher Hayes, Crown Publishing Group, Random House, New York, 2012.

www.ingramcontent.com/pod-product-compliance
Lightning Source LLC
LaVergne TN
LVHW051519080426
835509LV00017B/2104
9780991105304